CONTENTS

LIST OF ILLUSTRATIONS

ACKNOWLEDGEMENTS

"Separation and Memory" first appeared as Donfrancesco, F. (1980). "Separazione e memoria". In: F. Angeli (Ed.). *Dopo Jung*. Milan: Giuffrè.

"In the Garden of Venus" first appeared as Donfrancesco, F. (1989). "Mimesis". *Anima*; Donfrancesco, F. (1995). "Mimesis". *Harvest, 41*, n. 1.

"The Imaginal Action" first appeared as Donfrancesco, F. (1993). "L'azione immaginale". *Anima*.

"Towards a living Reality" first appeared as Donfrancesco, F. (1988). "L'insegnamento di un artista". *Anima*.

"Life inside Death" first appeared as "La vita nella morte". In: F. Donfrancesco. *Nello specchio di Psiche*. Bergamo: Moretti e Vitali, 1996.

"In the Interregnum" first appeared as Donfrancesco, F. (1999). "Nell'interregno". *Anima*.

"The Longing for a Mentor" first appeared as Donfrancesco, F. (1995). "L'opera del maestro". *Anima*; Donfrancesco, F. (1998). "The Longing for a Mentor". *Spring 63*.

"Unity in Multiplicity" first appeared as Donfrancesco, F. (2001). "Tutto è pieno di dèi". *Anima*.

"The Care of Art" first appeared as Donfrancesco, D. (2003). "La cura dell'arte". *Anima; "The Care of Art"*. In *Cambridge 2001: Proceedings of the Fifteenth International Congress for Analytical Psychology.* Einsiedeln: Daimon Verlag, 2003.

"Memory of the Invisible" first appeared as Zervas, D. F. and Donfrancesco, F. (2005). "Memoria dell'invisibile: Immagini del Nord e del Sud a confronto". *Anima*; "Memory of the Invisible". In *Barcelona 2004: Proceedings of the Sixteenth International Congress for Analytical Psychology. CD.*

PREFACE

The opportunity to edit this collection of Francesco Donfrancesco's essays has provided me with an occasion to close a circle. I first encountered his writing when I was asked to translate *Life inside Death* in 1996 for a conference he was giving in London the following spring. After many years as an art historian with an interest in Florentine renaissance art, I had recently qualified as a Jungian analyst, and although I was deeply interested in art and psychology, I was not yet ready to marry those two worlds. Then I began working, painstakingly, on Donfrancesco's moving piece. It was an activity akin to deep meditation, as I experienced Music's images, and their archetypal connections with the 'obscure places' of the human psyche that were revealed by Donfrancesco's loving circumambulation around them; weaving them into the artist's life and epoch, and into our souls, where we recognise and reconnect with them through Mnemosyne—memory—the daughter of Ouranos (Sky) and Gaia (Earth), who is the mediator between the soul and life in time.

Despite this experience, I did not meet Francesco Donfrancesco until a few years later. At that time, he lived with his family in the Tuscan countryside at Bagno a Ripoli, outside Florence. I well remember my surprise and delight at discovering that their simple *casa da compagna* was filled with modern works of art: still-lives, landscapes, portraits, suggestive images of people emerged from the shadows into limpid areas of light, which extended into his consulting room on the ground floor. These were images to be shared, not hoarded, with visitors and analysands, and many accompanied him when the family recently moved to the centre of Florence. Here Hermes is often constellated, as Francesco mischievously trades one work for another, or lovingly augments his living collection of art. In the hermetic container of his consulting room—which also serves as his study—they too bear silent witness to the intimate activity that we call analysis; encouraging creative engagement (or re-engagement) with the realm of images.

These memories and experiences constituted my own initiation into what Donfrancesco describes as 'soul-making', the subtle yet vital interweaving of art and analysis. His use of the word 'soul-making' is related—by way of archetypal psychologist James Hillman's use of the term—to Keats's description of the world as 'The vale of Soul-making' (Hillman 1983). What Donfrancesco intends by 'interweaving art and analysis' is far from a reductive explanation of the artist's work, as postulated by Freud, where art is reduced to the artist's neurosis, locked in his personal history. And it is subtly different from Jung's interest in art as the product of archetypal images released by the artist's unconscious and harnessed by him into tangible form, that speak autonomously through him, like thoughts unbidden, transformed into symbolic forms.

However, the warp of Donfrancesco's imaginal fabric is constructed from the same threads that often inspired and illuminated Freud and Jung: the potent gods, goddesses, myths and other living fragments of the Western classical world, eternally alive in what Jung called our 'prehistoric' matrix, the collective unconscious, as Francesco explains in *Separation and Memory*. When our egoic demands separate us from the memory of this matrix, the soul—anima—awakens Pothos—nostalgia—the desire to be reunited with the forgotten matrix, the fundament of images. If Pothos is misdirected towards the ideal and the future, anxiety, splitting, guilt and depression, coupled with exaltation, rebellious and authoritarian violence are released, and no interweaving can take place: we remain suspended, alienated from our life and our images. But if Pothos is allowed to follow its natural direction—towards Mnemosyne and her children, the artistic Muses—we are redirected towards the ancient realm of images. Then movement can take place, facilitating the creation of the symbol—*syn ballein*—the 'redeeming' psychic event that reconnects us with our imaginal world. The resultant forms—autobiographical, oneiric, analytic and artistic—make up the various coloured and textured threads of the weft that are woven on to the imaginal warp, creating the richly patterned tapestry of meanings and reality that constitute our lives.

As Donfrancesco reminds us again and again throughout these essays, art can stimulate memory, reflect back to us experiences perhaps long forgotten, capture a moment or a mood, and, by revealing previously hidden, primordial presences, can help to heal the suffering soul. Contemplating the creative synergy of the artist and his genius—his *daimon*—which imposes its vision on the artist and guides his hand, Donfrancesco evokes the ego-self axis, reminding us that the 'other' always exists, even if we are unaware of its presence. Loss of the 'other' is catastrophic, leaving the ego uncreative, reduced to hiding behind an imitative false self. Thus for Donfrancesco, healing in psychoanalysis is achieved by focusing on the expression of this *daimon*, thereby allowing new images to emerge into our time and space. It is the *daimon* who guides the weaver's hand, whose 'gnosis' intuitively 'knows' the design that will be produced in time; the ego comprehends this 'image darkly forming' knot by knot, on the back of the tapestry it is helping to weave.

Each essay takes us deeper and deeper into the fabric of the imaginal cloth. We reconnect with passages from famous classical texts, observe their invisible connections with Renaissance paintings, with the archetypal images underpinning later artists' works, and with the substructure of our soul. We linger with individual paintings by Fra Angelico, Botticelli, Vuillard, Bonnard, Morandi, Mattioli, and Music, plumbing their depths, allowing them to be, to speak, to move us, to reconnect us with ourselves. Through them we come to understand the importance of the multiplicity of images—*pan-demonium*—for the psyche. As Goethe's travelling companion, a Papal captain, remonstrated with Protestant Goethe on his journey to Rome in 1786: 'man should never limit himself to one thing only, otherwise one becomes crazy; it's essential to have a thousand things (*mille cose*), a confusion [of images] in one's head!' (Goethe 1970, p. 118). A monotheistic approach to images is pathological;

a polytheistic attitude is creative and healing. This theme—the cure of soul—is broadly explored by Donfrancesco in *Unity in Multiplicity*, and is related to the cure of art itself in our modern epoch, as he reminds us in *The Care of Art*.

Throughout the enriching work of editing these essays, one has been my constant companion: *The Longing for a Mentor*. As we become adults, we must leave our parental homes and parental images behind. If we do not, we project them on to the significant others we encounter; then we cannot grow into ourselves and we cannot meet 'the other'. The longing for a mentor, if followed with Pothos, connects us with a guide, one who initially may lead us towards new horizons. If we identify with this mentor, we lose ourselves again, or are shackled by the limitations of mimesis (from the Greek *mimeisthai*: the imitative representation of nature or human behaviour; the representation of another person's alleged words in a speech). If, on the other hand, we are truly mentored we are encouraged to explore, to grow at our own pace, to become ensouled, and to mentor others. In this respect, Donfrancesco and his writings have accompanied me—and will escort the reader—on this inspirational journey of discovery as we experience the fruitful interweaves between art and analysis.

Diane Finiello Zervas
London, July 2007

Introduction

The chapters of this book have been written over the course of many years and suggested by the frequentation of two places, both of them designed to reflect the images of the inner world, although in different ways: the analyst's studio and the painter's.

An interest in painting and poetry, and the particular slant on them that might be called the 'philology of the emotions', has preceded and to some extent shaped, even more than my medical studies, my approach to psychoanalysis, for it has been my means of access to the soul, or rather, to 'soul-making'. In more recent years, following the work of my painter friends, watching the appearance of unexpected images or the alteration of familiar ones, seeing their pictures before they are finished, recognizing in them the uncertainties, the changes of mind, sometimes even the signs of failure, and talking quietly about the teaching of the masters, cherishing their memory with devotion, has been a powerful lesson. This intimacy with the gestation of their paintings and with the dramatic aspects of their work has introduced me, in an almost tangible way, to the action of the Imaginal ego, as Hillman has called it, of that aspect of the ego complex that shares the life of images. In fact the imaginal ego is, like the artist, a mediator of images. It takes in their value and significance, translates them into the awareness of the ego, and allows this to look at the reality of the soul as a living entity, to experience it with the emotional warmth of the imagination.

Observing the work of those artists, and of others that I have studied, I have been able to see the slowness with which an image is usually brought into focus, attaining the precision of its form through trial and error, concealment and re-emergence. This is something that happens in analysis too, where we also find patient silence and listening, the long toil of uncertainty with the courage of faith. Bion must have been thinking of this parallel when he recommended to his pupils that they should approach analysis as if they were embarking on a work of art, or when he said that his interpretations would have been more effective if they had been able to stand up to aesthetic criticism. And Hillman was certainly thinking of it when he wrote, in 1981, in one of his essays on the colours of the soul: 'The poets and painters, and the figures in us who are poets and painters, are those struggling with the continuing alchemical problem: the transubstantiation of the material perspective into soul through ars, Artifex now artisan. The alchemical laboratory is in their work with words and paints, and psychology continues its tradition of learning from alchemy by learning from them. They tell us one further thing about the white earth: if the imaginal ground is first perceived by artistic method, then the very nature of this earth must be aesthetic—the way is the goal. We come to the white ground when our way of doing psychology is aesthetic. An aesthetic psychology, a psychology whose muse is anima, is already hesitantly moving, surely moving, in that white place' (Hillman 1993, p.143).

The movement foreseen by Hillman—and in those same years followed in different and independent ways by some of Bion's pupils, like Meltzer in *The Apprehension of Beauty* really is possible if it is sustained by a reflection capable of interweaving art and analysis in a structural rather than sporadic manner, something that is feasible if the common foundation for both is acknowledged in the soul. This prospect emerges spontaneously when we go back to the classical, Neoplatonic conception of art, which recognizes in images the power of the memory to connect and even unify the meaning of psychological and cultural experiences that are remote from one another. Warburg, whose thinking ran along similar lines to that of Jung, has demonstrated that images have the power to form and transform mentality. Thus it becomes possible to look at the analytical experience with the eye of the artist and at artistic imagination with the eye of the psychoanalyst, picking out their analogies without straining them, and following the spontaneous shifts from one plane to another, from one language to another.

The image of which I am speaking is an autonomous organism, a 'presence' that belongs to a median and mediating order of reality, and reveals both the process through which it is constituted and remains alive and the purpose that is inherent in it: the transformation of the events of time into timeless forms. Thus it carries out a commemoration, and for this reason the ancients assigned its origin to Mnemosyne, the archetypal memory in whose crucible the fluid formlessness of events attains a stable form, and a detail of the cosmos is brought to light. The manifestation of this reunion was called 'beauty' by the Platonists, and the evocation of beauty was seen as the responsibility of art; not beauty as a characteristic that can be reified and identified by a canon of taste, but as expression of the independent interweaving of time and eternity in a mediating image.

When beauty is manifested in the world, as the Neoplatonic myth of Cupid and Psyche tells us, it stirs and attracts the passion of Eros, pointing the way to the dark areas of the soul. Eros will then be able to carry out his function of symbolizing, of bringing the personal back to the archetypal, the human to the divine. And the foundations of the language of myth will be laid, permitting us to recognize individual experiences, even the most painful and humiliating ones, as common, shared and worthy of our love and compassion.

I wrote each of these chapters with the aim of finding a suitable form for my most intense fantasies of the moment; and it is with the same intention that I went back to what had already been published, whenever it seemed to me that I had gained a better understanding of what I had once begun to discern and to define. I am reminded of what Henri Matisse wrote of his work: he said that a painting, if it is going to last, cannot just contain the feelings of one moment; it is necessary to go back to it so that the complex, polymorphic life of the soul has the time to deposit itself on the canvas. Thus he never hurried to finish a picture in the evening, but left its incompleteness as an open wound from which he could recommence the next day. Doesn't this sound like a metaphor for the work of analysis? And even of analytical writing, at least as I understand it: an expression of processes underway in the author's soul, a sort of active imagination.

Slowness is necessary to the imaginal ego because it is necessary to the feeling with which it discerns particular configurations as well as different intensities, and because the terrain on which it moves, the inner space of images, is the most vulnerable, the part most deeply touched by pain. In fact it is precisely its continuity with images and emotions that allows it to be caught up in the drama of the passions. This is also why it is that aspect of the ego which draws it not only into the most profound feelings of joy, but also into those of suffering. So when the wounds and sufferings of the soul become unbearable, the imaginal ego is repressed, as a last defence, and with it the true imagination, the one capable of lending spiritual substance to emotions and passions, of making them the memory and expression of an inner cosmos. In this way, that precious aspect of the life of the soul that is entrusted to the imaginal ego is lost, in order quell the devastation.

The imaginal ego is sensitive to the disclosure of living reality as image, to the beauty that arises in our opening up to being something which happens when we do not avoid the pathos that permeates the soul of the world. There are artists who are better than others at conveying this intimate relationship between pathos, beauty and world, and their self-portraits are perhaps the best representations of the imaginal ego: those of Rembrandt serve as examples, almost 'archetypes'.

There are only a few places where Hillman mentions the imaginal ego, and yet the importance of this metaphor in his thinking is evident. Hillman has avoided treating it like a substance, a 'thing', as can occur when a metaphor is reduced to a concept to make it easier to communicate; instead he has chosen to move from the perspective of the imaginal ego itself, allowing it to exist and reveal itself in all its complexity in so many of the pages that he has written. For the same reasons, it is preferable for the poetics of analysis, which run through the pages of this book like a watermark, not to be reduced to a declaration of intent, but to manifest itself indirectly, showing through the words.

From this perspective, the analytical experience looks like a peculiar process of imagination, a poiesis, a 'making' generated in the intimacy of individual encounters; a transmutation of the infinite particularities, carried out by the memory in accordance with unconscious archetypal patterns. And when a written 'memoir', a 'theory', stems from this, it too will be an expression of imaginal action and an exercise in listening to the soul. If on the other hand this reflection were to present itself as an objective mirror and 'scientific' interpretation of the analytical experience, then it would end up colluding with that compulsion to control, to exercise power, that already for Freud constituted the 'stony ground of neurosis', the first matrix of a never-ending analysis.

I feel that the poetics of analysis is expressed as psychopoiesis, in that process of soul-making which breaks down the defensive isolation in which the ego's awareness has found itself trapped, and that allows it, by recovering the lost imaginal sense, to attain truly the living reality of which it is part, its pain, its violence, its joy: a patient exercise of attention and compassion which sets free, in the emotional content, a memory of light, of beauty. Then the passions begin to be experienced and seen no longer solely as a source of instability and anxiety, but as a necessary way for the soul to 'descend' and take on form in the world of the senses, involving individual and world in this descent and binding them together. And their violence will appear to be a consequence of the soul's need to make its way into the world, even if this means breaking down every resistance, every pre-existing state, in order to make a breach. As the imaginal sense contained in the passions gains ground, they are subdued, undergoing a slow twisting, a metamorphosis through which the particular, personal character of their goals is attenuated and the living Idea inside them starts to emerge, revealing themselves as original and originating presences. We could also say, with Marcel Proust, that every person who makes us suffer or rather, every set of images and emotions which that person represents in our existenceis revealed in the end as a fragmentary reflection, leading to a 'divinity (Idea) the contemplation of whom...will give us immediate happiness instead of our former pain (Proust, *Time Regained*, pp. 250-251). Or rather, he or she makes joy sprout from sadness, as the return from exile has found its fulfilment.

From this viewpoint, analysis can also turn to the art of its own time, commencing a dialogue in which the practice of analysis and the practice of art can illuminate and assist one another by devoting their attention to the same task: nurturing the memory concealed in the passions and allowing it to surface in time, linking time to eternity, the end to the beginning.

I should like to thank James Hillman, to whose ideas my thoughts are unreservedly linked from the initial draft of the first of these chapters; the editor Enrico Moretti, for permission to use the articles published in the periodical *Anima*, which for the last ten years has relied on his responsive and precious support; and Renos Papadopoulos, for his enthusiasm and encouragement to make my writings known in the United Kingdom.

A particularly warm word of thanks is owed to Diane Finiello Zervas, who has edited this book with intelligence and sensitivity, and with an attention that only a live friendship is capable of sustaining; without her *Soul-Making* could perhaps have been conceived, but certainly would not have seen the light.

Florence, July 2007

CHAPTER ONE

Separation and Memory

In his old age, Jung decided to bring out a new edition of the book that had marked his split with Freud in 1912. And so, forty years later, *Wandlungen und Symbole der Libido* (published in English in 1916 as *Psychology of the Unconscious*) became *Symbole der Wandlung* (*Symbols of Transformation*). When we compare the two versions, we find omissions and new sentences in the new edition; certain terms have vanished and others, taken from later works, have been added, and the original meaning seems to have shifted, almost imperceptibly, revealing a layer that previously was only implied. Thus we marvel when we come to passages in which we think we recognize the hand of the later Jung, so great is their authority, only to find that they are also in the first version, word for word; passages that seem definitive, like thoughts mulled over at length and set as the seal on a life of study, but which were, in fact, its seeds. For example, the solemn opening words of the book:

> Anyone who can read Freud's *Interpretation of Dreams* without being outraged by the novelty and seemingly unjustified boldness of his procedure, and without waxing morally indignant over the stark nudity of his dream-interpretations, but can let this extraordinary book work upon his imagina-

tion calmly and without prejudice, will not fail to be deeply impressed at that point where Freud reminds us that an individual conflict, which he calls the incest fantasy, lies at the root of that monumental drama of the ancient world, the Oedipus legend. The impression made by this simple remark may be likened to the uncanny feeling which would steal over us if, amid the noise and bustle of a modern city street, we were suddenly to come upon an ancient relic—say the Corinthian capital of a long-immured column, or a fragment of an inscription. A moment ago, and we were completely absorbed in the hectic, ephemeral life of the present; then, the next moment, something very remote and strange flashes upon us, which directs our gaze to a different order of things. We turn away from the vast confusion of the present to glimpse the higher continuity of history. Suddenly we remember that on this spot where we now hasten to and fro about our business a similar scene of life and activity prevailed two thousand years ago in slightly different forms; similar passions moved mankind, and people were just as convinced as we are of the uniqueness of their lives. This is the impression that may very easily be left behind by a first acquaintance with the monuments of antiquity, and it seems to me that Freud's reference to the Oedipus legend is in every way comparable. While still struggling with the confusing impressions of the infinite variability of the individual psyche, we suddenly catch a glimpse of the simplicity and grandeur of the Oedipus tragedy, that perennial highlight of the Greek theatre. This broadening of our vision has about it something of a revelation. (Jung 1956, par. 1)

The enthusiasm that Jung expresses in this passage invites us to take a look at another, in the *Interpretation of Dreams*, with which it forms an ideal diptych:

There must be something which makes a voice within us ready to recognize the compelling force of destiny in the *Oedipus*.... His destiny moves us only because it might have been ours—because the oracle laid the same curse upon us before our birth as upon him.

It is the fate of all of us, perhaps, to direct our first sexual impulse toward our mother and our first hatred and our first murderous wish against our father. Our dreams convince us that this is so. King Oedipus, who slew his father Laius and

> married his mother Jocasta, merely shows us the fulfilment of our own childhood wishes. But, more fortunate than he, we have meanwhile succeeded, in so far as we have not become psychoneurotics, in detaching our sexual impulses from our mothers and in forgetting our jealousy of our fathers. Here is one in whom these primeval wishes of our childhood have been fulfilled, and we shrink back from him with the whole force of the repression by which those wishes have since that time been held down within us. While the poet, as he unravels the past, brings to light the guilt of Oedipus, he is at the same time compelling us to recognize our own inner minds, in which those same impulses, though suppressed, are still to be found. The contrast with which the closing Chorus leaves us confronted—
>
> [...] Fix on Oedipus your eyes, Who resolved the dark enigma, noblest champion and most wise. Like a star his envied fortune mounted beaming far and wide: Now he sinks in seas of anguish, whelmed beneath a raging tide [...]
>
> – strikes as a warning at ourselves and our pride, at us who since our childhood have grown so wise and so mighty in our own eyes. (Freud 1900a, pp. 262-63).

Both passages tell us that an appearance has been shattered, that the surface has irreversibly given way, for our gaze has now reached another reality and an ancient relic has re-emerged, the present and past have been joined: a connection destined to become the crucial point from which, within a short space of time, the differences between Freud and Jung would become ever greater.

As we continue reading *Psychology of the Unconscious,* we find illuminating metaphors: a gulf is bridged, and existence, which seemed fragmentary, discontinuous and fortuitous, suddenly reveals a unifying ground, the persistence of one and the same reality at different places and times:

> ... then the gulf that separates our age from antiquity is bridged over, and we realize with astonishment that Oedipus is still alive for us. The importance of this realization should not be underestimated, for it teaches us that there is an identity of fundamental human conflicts which is independent of time and place. What aroused a feeling of horror in the Greeks still remains true, but it is true for us only if we give up the

vain illusion that we are *different*, i.e., morally better, than the ancients (Jung 1956, par. 1).

This is the point at which Jung had encountered Freud, only to distance himself shortly afterwards, for it was here that he found the decisive subject of his research, one that caused the collapse of an illusion, and at the same time allowed a new vision to emerge. Freud, on the other hand, viewed the effects of that same collapse in reductive terms ('it is only this'), bitterly presenting himself as the one who knows the truth, while others still delude themselves: 'Like Oedipus, we live in ignorance of the desires that offend morality, the desires that nature has forced upon us and after their unveiling we may well prefer to avert our gaze from the scenes of our childhood' (Freud 1900a, p. 263). Just as Jung, in his view, continued to do, having devised another way to avert his eyes from reality. Freud hinted at this in a note added to this passage in the 1914 edition, after the publication of Jung's book: 'An attempt has even been made recently to make out, in the face of all experience, that the incest should only be taken as "symbolic"' (Freud 1900a, p. 263n); and as his 'only' demonstrates, for Freud 'symbolic' denotes 'unreal'.

If we are unable to gain access to reality through symbolic forms, then we will be forced to seek its origins in the childhood history of the individual, and the ultimate reality that we wish to uncover will be found in infantile drives and their vicissitudes. If infantile drives have this character of fundamental reality, not just personal history but also the history of humanity and the development of its culture will have to be understood from the beginning—according to the principle that ontology recapitulates phylogeny—because the veil of illusions has now been rent, throwing 'a light of undreamt-of-importance on the history of the human race and the evolution of religion and morality' (Freud 1900a, 263n). Hence while Jung wrote *Psychology of the Unconscious*, Freud wrote *Totem and Taboo* (1912-13), his anthropogeny: this occurred at the outset of human evolution, when the drives had their naked epiphany but also began to be tamed, the work of culture.

All cultural history would thus reflect the need to domesticate, sublimate and forget infantile drives and their consequences. Therefore Freud and his followers set out to rewrite history and the human sciences, beginning from this primal event which had hitherto been ignored, unmasking any cultural formation as illusion, defence or sublimation; and they sought to break down, reconstruct and reinterpret the history of each individual, whatever his or her human accomplishment, on the basis of the structuring of infantile drives. Analysis, in turn, would become the ritual of the return to one's origins, a setting in which to repeat the experience of that reality in transference and recognize it, separating it from the present in order to be able to forget it.

If we look at where Jung reveals his emotion, however, we find him concentrating on something else: infantile drives are not neglected, but they are not considered the foundation of psychic life, since the other reality, the ultimate and unshakable object of his interest, lies beyond childhood and any personal events, not in individual or collective history but in their 'prehistoric' matrix. Jung too was excited by the irruption of the past into the present, but the eternally present past, which was there before the individual existed and was aware of himself—'something very remote and strange flashes upon us, which directs our gaze to a different order of things. We turn away from the vast confusion of the present to glimpse the higher continuity of history'. This 'remote and strange', which also appears in our dreams, is significant of a 'different order', the order of the soul, and the illusion that concealed the reality of the soul from our eyes is due to the 'slightly different forms' by which 'people were just as convinced as we are of the uniqueness of their lives'.

For Freud, forgetting concerned the personal experience of infantile drives. Jung discovered instead—through Freud's own writing—that 'an indissoluble link binds us to the men of antiquity' (Jung 1956, par. 1); and this 'different order' to which his gaze was drawn was a means of reconciliation for him. In fact, Jung's emotion was only due to the revelation of a new possibility of understanding, of establishing 'a firm foothold outside our own culture from which alone it is possible to gain an objective understanding of its foundations' (Jung 1956, par. 1); but it was above all therapeutic emotion. The 'firm foothold outside our own culture', the 'indissoluble link', heals us from rootless, unconnected individuality, from the isolation that Jung identified as the essential characteristic of mental suffering: 'If this supra-individual psyche exists, everything that is translated into its picture-language would be depersonalized, and if this became conscious would appear to us *sub specie aeternitatis*. Not as my sorrow, but as the sorrow of the world; not a personal isolating pain, but a pain without bitterness that unites all humanity. The healing effect of this needs no proof' (Jung 1931a,7, par. 316).

'Oedipus is still alive': this was the reason for Jung's astonishment. Breaking through the forgetting of incestuous impulses and their consequences had led him to dissolve an ontological forgetting: that the history of the individual is a weft woven into a warp of myth. The ancient relic in the noise and bustle of a city street changes things; its presence is so decisive that from that street and that bustle another reality now emerges, and is interwoven with the immediate appearance. Jung later gave the name 'collective unconscious' to this presence, which gives meaning and duration to 'the confusing impressions of the infinite variability of the individual psyche' and recognized its manifestations above all in those powerfully charged images where the soul's action is intensified, and its value transcends the sphere of the individual.

The ancient relic, this fundamental metaphor, helps us to understand why Jung connected the generating and moulding centres of the collective unconscious with archaic representations, and why he called them 'archetypes': in fact the soul often makes itself known with a quality of the past, and becomes conscious of itself as 'memory'. This memory, which can be said in turn to be 'archetypal', is the mediator between the soul and life in time: it orients the time of the individual, since it inscribes it in a pre-existing mythical or ritual form; it stirs religious feelings, which reassemble fortuitous and fragmentary events into a harmonious and meaningful whole; and it is the guide to a remote presence from which the present emanates a lasting, eternal, unknown and yet certain reality.

Jung first called archetypes 'a priori forms of intuition' (Jung [1916]/1957, par. 133), and then 'the inborn possibilities of ideas' (Jung 1931a,3, par. 126). In other words, he conceived them as configurations pre-existent to the ego, a memory that guides the ego by pointing out its manifestations: '... a dark impulse is the ultimate arbiter of the pattern, an unconscious *a priori* precipitates itself into plastic form .... Over the whole procedure there seems to reign a dim foreknowledge not only of the pattern but of its meaning' (Jung 1954b,2: par. 402).

So the soul is the place of origin, the inviolable and remote foundation that manifests itself as memory while we return to it. It is characteristic of this memory to give a mythical, archaic form to images, which are therefore not pre-existing forms, permanent in us and handed down literally as if they were substances, but an expression of a latent memory, which for us and in them evokes our antiquity, the mythical warp of our histories. This memory is the force that gives foundation to our existences, as well as to the common history of human beings; and it is because of the eclipse of memory that we become incapable of giving suitable names and meanings, being disoriented and lost or vainly deluded, because the names and meanings that give life and succour to the individual come from the soul. For this reason, the soul and name of the individual coincide (Jung 1933a,9, par. 665), and the name is a metaphor for the soul.

Between the ego, in which individuality is made manifest, and its foundation, the soul, from which it emerges, a third party has inserted itself from the beginning, and still exists, the Separator—the serpent of the Garden of Eden, the devil (*diaballein*), which has divided what was united. This is what establishes the dominion of Time, of Kronos, that separates Heaven and Earth forever, which fragments unity, the original and originating embrace, generating the irreducible duality (Jung 1948a,4, par. 248), and ontological forgetting. The 'prince of the world' binds to the world—which is considered diabolic matter for the *diaballein* in which it is revealed—and, as Lucifer, brings light, the knowledge of individuality, of being individuals, and of the separateness and singleness in which the reality of the world is revealed. But this light, the little light of one of Jung's dreams, renders invisible and forgotten what is not described in its field, the reality of the soul, which owing to the separation is not seen as immediate, but transpires in the world as memory. Memory is the 'eternal return', the 'repetition' that bridges the distance, the gulf, but without cancelling it out.

Anxiety stems from the absence of memory, when separation has created an unfathomable gap, and one side has moved so far away that nothing reaches it. Nothing is perceived but the dark cleft and the vertigo of the precipice over which we have stretched in vain. This is the 'loss of the soul', and it makes us feel empty, lost and in exile, guilty over our complicity with the separating serpent, no longer having any memory of the source of life—but there is another possibility that should not be forgotten, the insufficient presence of the ego, i.e. the flaw of separation and singleness... (Jung 1954b,2, par. 430). And the source of personal life, the mother who gave birth to us and suckled us, whom we have loved and sought, she who was there before we existed and desired our birth, who knew of us before we knew...; she who knows and remembers, who seduces us, and for whom our hearts are consumed with yearning, herself becomes mythical and metaphorical—a metaphor for the soul—and any interpretation that sets out to constrain her within its personal dimension in the end leaves us bewildered and disappointed, at the mercy of a loss that seems irretrievable, for it exposes us even more to the silence of memory.

Jung gave a Latin name, 'anima', to the presence that tells the ego something is missing and that, by exciting in it a yearning for the origins, makes it desire and seek the lost source personified by the mother. The call of the anima, from the other side of the abyss, awakes Pothos, the desire that is not satisfied by what is tangible and present, that longs for that from which it has been separated, and that heads towards the mythical destinations of boundless journeys; or, since nothing conjures up the unattainable like the past, advances towards the lost shores of memory.

The most common way of responding to the appeal of the anima is the falling in love prompted by Pothos: the passionate love that lasts for as long as the *numen* that irradiates life and soul everywhere, and that bears the scent of the long awaited unknown, is seen in the beloved. The deeper the gulf and the stronger Pothos, the more elated and blind is the passion: thus we can understand why the most enduring loves are nurtured by distance (and by loss and rejection), and why they are renewed or inflamed for the unattainable analyst. They have the force of an eternity, of an apparition and a revelation, or of an event fixed in memory as a definitive gesture, and so announce a reality that persists and comes to us from outside time. The image that we cultivate and desire without any hope of satisfaction is in fact the illusory simulacrum of the anima. And when in dreams the presence of the beloved gives us a fleeting feeling of complete happiness, or when we make out in the crowd, with a start, a face or a smile that for a moment reminds us of the person who is 'faraway' or 'lost', these are the moments in which a veiled anima comes to us, the *kairoi* that rend the opaque continuity of time and through which the longed-for reality is fleetingly glimpsed.

The metaphor of the 'ancient relic' is not just an apt rhetorical device. In fact, reading C.G. Jung's *Memories, Dreams, Reflections,* we find its origin in a dream that was so significant for Jung that he considered it a prelude to *Psychology of the Unconscious*:

> 'I was in a house I did not know, which had two storeys. It was "my house". I found myself in the upper storey where there was a kind of salon furnished with fine pieces in rococo style. On the walls hung a number of precious old paintings; I wondered that this should be my house, and thought "Not bad!" But then it occurred to me that I did not know what the lower floor looked like. Descending the stairs, I reached the ground floor. There everything was much older, and I realised that this part of the house must date from about the 15th

> or 16th century. The furnishings were medieval; the floors were of red brick. Everywhere was rather dark. I went from one room to another, thinking "Now I really must explore the whole house". I came upon a heavy door and opened it. Beyond it, I discovered a stone stairway that led down into the cellar. Descending again, I found myself in a beautifully vaulted room which looked exceedingly ancient. Examining the walls, I discovered layers of brick among ordinary stone blocks, and chips of bricks and mortar. As soon as I saw this I knew that the walls were dated from Roman times. My interest by now was intense. I looked more closely at the floor. It was of stone slabs, and in one I discovered a ring. When I pulled it, the stone slab lifted, again I saw a stairway of narrow stone steps leading down into the depths. These, too, I descended and entered a low cave cut into the rock. Thick dust lay on the floor, and in the dust were scattered bones and broken pottery, like the remains of a primitive culture. I discovered two human skulls, obviously very old and half-disintegrated' (Jung 1963, pp.182-83).

Like the evocation of Oedipus, the dream, which he commented on with Freud, marked a crossroads, the transitory and unexpected intersection of two ways. Jung himself would make use of the metaphor of the crossroads when he described the phenomena of transference in 1946: the crossroads as the place where two ways get mixed up, since dissimilarity and separation seem to vanish there owing to the irruption of the 'same' into the 'different'. The halt at the crossroads, where difference appears to give way to a state of identity, can generate an intensified erotic intimacy, but it can also produce a violent antagonism (a struggle to divide, the work of 'Satan', the 'Adversary', the separating devil) in order to regain independence through a breaking away, and even a fantasy of annihilation. This happens because it is perceived as a violation of the boundaries of the ego, as terrifying or humiliating (or even seductive, another danger), in other words a threat to the autonomy of the ego due to the pervasive influence of the anima, mediator of the unknown; even if the anima appears in the guise of the other, who for this reason, and perhaps only for this reason, takes on a disturbing demonic character.

Jung's account describes an exemplary case of two-way resistance. Freud, the analyst, puts up a marked resistance to the reawakening of memory, to its eruption as a result of the relationship, and so reduces the images, in which the soul is revealed to him, to personal and 'secret death wishes'—following a model of interpretation that tends to reinforce the independence of the ego, which is weakened by the dream because it takes the ego into the more profound space of the soul. The person analyzed, in his turn, feels a 'violent resistance to any such interpretation', but at the same time fears the personal consequences of his opposition, and feigns submission, placating the analyst's by 'saying something that suited his theories', and thus relieving his anxiety (Jung 1963, p. 183). We can imagine a patient in these circumstances left alone, secretly cultivating images that go unheard, that are not accepted, and who, less able and determined than Jung and more unconscious of himself, redoubles and reinforces the original dissociation, the ontological forgetting, in the transference, identifying him or herself with the aggressor. Some patients come to understand—although this does not often happen, even during training in analysis—the degree to which they can be hated, the skill with which they can be dismissed as pathological and kept at a distance, because the analyst is unable to overcome his separation from the soul, and thus yields to the imaginary threat of a dissolution of the ego in the soul. Perhaps psychoanalysis has become, as Freud said, 'an instrument to enable the ego to achieve a progressive conquest of the id' (Freud 1923b, p. 56), in order to foster an ever more marked separation from the soul, and for this reason destined to appear increasingly dangerous and 'overwhelming': '[The object of] the therapeutic efforts of psychoanalysis... is to strengthen the ego ... so ... that it can appropriate fresh portions of the id.... It is a work of culture— not unlike the draining of the Zuider Zee' (Freud 1933a, p. 80). All this with the elaboration of complex systems of interpretation, which are the tools of this 'work of culture', of its act of 'draining', and considering dreams, that attract one to the soul, as deceptions to be unmasked through interpretation.

The attitude is quite different if the soul is regarded as the decisive value, the fundamental reality: then the images are seen as a direct manifestation of it, to be understood as presences and events in their own right and not to be interpreted as mere symbols, hieroglyphs to be deciphered. With them one lives, observes, learns, examines and acts in that reality and one reacts to it, evaluating, contemplating, exploring, loving, fearing: one thing does not stand for another, it is not a murky language that needs translating into the limpid one of the ego. The attempt to integrate (or rather to incorporate) the reality of the soul into the ego, to the point of nullifying it, is above all the reflection of an underlying sense of desperation.

The soul reveals itself in narrations, where it can take the form of landscape, nature, home, god and goddess, daemons, lovers, wise or wicked old men. These stories, humble or grand, interweaving and disentangling continually, are the reality in which we live, just as we inhabit the reality of the world. And reality is stronger than we are: it moves us, it defines us. Yet this fact does not authorize us to consider 'this same ego as a poor creature owing service to three masters and consequently menaced by three dangers: from the external world, from the libido of the id, and from the severity of the super-ego' (1923b, p. 56). Threatened in this way, the ego is what Jung would call an autonomous complex. What is expressed in this description, rather, is the anxiety of a 'heroic' ego, caught between the promise of domination and impending bondage by its scission from the soul (and from an animate world), and by the duty of a 'progressive conquest of the id', i.e. the reduction of any otherness to a subjective, dominated form.

Let us go back now to Jung's dream and his commentary on it. The burning questions that he had asked himself in the days preceding the dream were the conceptual form of his yearning for the soul; and in the dream the soul was revealed in a form that became 'a guiding image which in the days to come was to be corroborated to an extent I could not at first suspect' (Jung 1963, p.185). What most interests us here are some decisive effects that the dream had on him: '... it revived my old interest in archaeology. I ... read various works on myths ....It was as if I were in an imaginary madhouse and were beginning to treat and analyse all the centaurs, nymphs, gods and goddesses in Creuzer's book as though they were my patients...' (Jung 1963, p.186). In other words it was memory that he had rediscovered through that dream, and this was precisely why it became a guiding image for Jung.

If we turn our attention not just to what Jung looked at in the dream, but also to himself, to his emotions, his method of observing, his movements, then we can recognize the emergence of memory in his actions, in the way he walked through its rooms, something of which Augustine had spoken in book X of the *Confessions*. Similarly, the subsequent reawakening of his interest in archaeology and myth was a realization of the neoplatonic *epistrophe*—the recollection ruled by Mnemosyne and her daughters the Muses—through which particular historical events find form, meaning and reality by creating symbols with the myths to which they are traced back, and personal pathologies with the *infirmitas* of archetypes. A movement that can take place—as Proclus wrote in his hymn to the Muses, and as we have seen in Jung—'by sacred rites from books that rouse the mind' with ancient stories, that 'teach to hasten o'er deep Lethe's wave'.

If we compare this with other dreams, we will find it easier to track down and describe at least some of the symbols that recur in the reawakening of memory. To begin with, the perception of an 'unknown' that arouses our interest, because it concerns us in some way. In this dream of Jung's, as in others that resemble it, the unknown is nevertheless 'my house': sometimes the dreamer is already in it, and at others arrives there after a walk. The character of memory can be conveyed through the vague sensation of having already been in that place, even though it is unfamiliar, as well as through its ancient appearance.

A young woman, for example, related this dream:

> I was walking with my companion along a winding path that climbed gently up the hill. There were no trees or vegetation, just vast fields of yellow grass. We arrived at an isolated farmhouse, almost on top of the hill, and entered the large kitchen, which was the centre of the house. There a couple of peasants looked at us in silence; I was particularly aware of the presence of the woman, who had the appearance of a housewife. There was a large and ancient fireplace, completely blackened by centuries of fire: it was so black that I couldn't see the back of it. I felt that it was very deep, of a black and unknown depth. The rest of the house was old too, almost primitive; the floor was of packed earth. There were a few benches, a table, a few essential and crudely made pieces of crockery. The inside of the house was much older than the outside suggested. In this place there was the sensation of living in a different, and yet familiar time: like a return. After looking carefully at the whole of the room, I found myself alone with my companion: the man and woman seemed to have vanished. That would have been our house.

The unknown often reveals itself through images of the past, which grab our attention: as if we have come across them in the course of a journey, an exploration or a restoration that has removed the layers covering an ancient fresco that had previously been invisible; or through an intense gaze into darkness, until an image slowly emerges, with a clarity that disperses the shadows. The 'thing', the image in which it is now made visible, was always there, as if waiting for someone to unveil it: a pre-existent place of history and stories. Not a chance meeting-place, but my house, the house where I will live, a foundation on which I can set down roots. They are images that allow us to imagine, and at times evoke essential thoughts, wise words, an illuminating or disconcerting paradox.

Our interest is often stirred gradually: a detail emerges unexpectedly in an indistinct scene and seizes our attention. And then it is as if the gaze, focusing intensely on the detail and wishing to explore and discover, sees the field expand, with the appearance of other objects and places, so that the initial detail is caught in a web of richer and more meaningful connections. More often the process is discontinuous: it is only when the perception is complete and, above all, our interest totally absorbed, that the visual field expands to include another set of images, as if a level of attention had reached saturation point. This process can occur in just one place, going from the detail to the whole; or, as in Jung's dream, in the form of a movement from one room to another, after carefully examining and getting to know the first.

Another typical expression of the unknown that stirs our interest is the journey of exploration, which sometimes starts out in the more banal form of a tourist trip and then, through the appearance of specific signs that catch and absorb the attention, and that isolate the traveller from others, unexpectedly turns into 'my journey'. Then it is possible to find a trace, a sign, an evocation or a map which tells me that this, even though I did not know it, had been my journey from the outset, and the places found or rediscovered were the ones I was looking for: '... and then something very remote and strange flashes upon us, which directs our gaze to a different order ...'.

This awareness is not an intention of the ego. On the contrary, we have the feeling of being distracted from something else that is engaging our attention, of an interference with our initial orientation, on the part of something of whose existence we had no suspicion: 'something directs our gaze'. It is a 'turning away from', a shifting of our attention from our habitual and everyday condition, from the usual connections; like the beginning of a journey of exploration, when 'we turn away', sometimes even with sorrow, or fear. Something is revealed and attracts our gaze, distracting us 'from the vast confusion of the present': there is a feeling of surprise, wonder, discovery, and the perception of a discontinuity in the passing of time, a caesura, expressed with 'suddenly', or 'unexpectedly', or with a hiatus in the scene of the action—a change or a forgetting of all the previous action.

A dream related by a man over the course of a long analysis describes one of these endless journeys, one of these amazed explorations, without beginning or end, with only partial maps:

> I was in a wood and walking along a path. I realized that near the path, on my right, there was a large colonnaded temple, and from the appearance of the stone I was certain it was Roman; I though it was a place colonized by the Romans. Beyond the temple I discovered first an amphitheatre, and then the *cavea* of a theatre. At this point I knew that there were the ruins of a fourth building, but one that I couldn't see, perhaps in a valley below. I knew that it was an archaic construction, of much earlier date than the Roman ones and, unlike these, built by the primitive indigenous population. Then I continued along the path, which was overgrown with vegetation like the ancient ruins. I stopped at a point higher up, turned around and tried to make out the archaic building, which I couldn't see but was able to imagine, as if I had seen a similar work of architecture elsewhere. For the first time I had the sensation of being on a journey. At this point, perhaps, I started to tell someone close to me about an experience I had had. The images of this recollection grew so intense and clear that I felt as if they were actually present. I was on the deck of a boat. Leaning on a bulwark, I observed the coast along which the boat was sailing. It had the appearance of a desert, with large and craggy rocks and no trace of vegetation. The light and heat of the sun were intense and the sky was clear: the rocks that had attracted my attention seemed to be made of sandstone, and there were no shady areas between them, as when the sun is at its zenith. I was fascinated by this place and looked carefully at the big rocks, their forms, their colours. All of a sudden, a great isolated column appeared among the rocks: I was astonished. It was a rock just like the ones around it, but bore the signs of human intervention; as if in ancient times some men had found this rock, which had a naturally cylindrical shape, and worked it to turn it into a column. The presence of this column made the whole coast intensely interesting to me. I peered carefully at the rocks, which continued to pass in front of me, and looked for other traces of an ancient human presence. Columns like the first appeared, more

> and more frequently and closer together. Suddenly, in a sandy hollow that opened up among the rocks, I saw a large number of columns grouped together, and on top of some of them I saw ancient religious symbols. One in particular caught my eye: it was a cross with arms the same length, very broad and thin and with rounded ends, as if it were inscribed in a virtual circle. I had the certainty that what I was seeing was a natural, archaic temple. Then I had the "magical" sensation that the cross, the other religious symbols and the columns were all looking in one direction, towards a faraway and indefinite point: they were looking in the literal sense, as if they were alive, with silent and sentient concentration. I felt like joining them and looking at that distant point too, oblivious of everything. I was back on the path in the wood: the recollection had been so intense that there had been no sense of time passing, and it was as if I were still trying to glimpse the archaic ruin; but now I knew where I had seen the architecture that I had thought I was imagining. I showed my travelling companion, who asked me what was going on, the point where we were on a map. It was a map that I didn't know I had and that I now used with confidence: one part of the route we were following was traced on it. We were in Africa, at the point that is closest to the southern tip of Arabia. I drew two opposing angles, which almost touched at the apex: they represented the areas of the two unknown regions on our journey. The coast seen from the boat was Arabian; the Roman colony was on the coast opposite, in Africa.

As the memory of 'a work of culture', the character of an ancient Roman garrison possessed by the present-day scene in the dream brought the civilizing power of the ego back to its mythical foundation. And the invisible archaic ruin was not an incidental vestige, but a fourth construction connected with the three Roman ones, with which it formed a whole; and at the same time it was the element that destabilized the whole, because it broke the continuity in time, revealing an interruption, a 'before' and an 'after'. It was precisely by this otherness that the forgetfulness was dissolved, the gap was bridged, and what had seemed a casual walk now proved to have a history, a route and a map. The effects on the traveller were already perceived in the dream: before the archaic ruin reawakened the traveller's memory, he was moving as if at random, in waking as in dream, aware of what immediately caught his attention and roused his wonder, but remaining conscious only of disconnected fragments. After the memory was revealed in a progression of images, which the dream seemed to bring together and render even clearer, the fragments assembled themselves into an itinerary that could be shared and made known to others—to the analyst, to start with. The itinerary was already present, but hitherto unconscious. Reflecting the map in the drawing, and giving a clear and concise form to the places in the drawing, making it comprehensible to a fellow traveller, was a metaphor for the new state of awareness, when it was found to be steeped and rooted in memory.

This dream can also help us to identify Jung's therapeutic metaphor, the *syn ballein*, which for him was the 'redeeming' psychic event—as he defined it from *Psychological Types* onward. In the dream, an arm of the sea separates one shore from the other, the place of a memory of the unknowable eternal and that of a discriminating consciousness oriented towards domination of the world, and yet mythical too. So the path of exploration that the map reflects is the experience of a distinction and a connection: right shore and left shore, emerging planes and subterranean planes, joint goals of an exploration that is itself *syn ballein*.

In this dream, as in the others examined here, there is the perception of an itinerary, explicit or virtual, which is never known beforehand, and is discovered as it is followed, without the place of origin and the goal being clear. The rare occasions on which the dreamer arrives in a place that seems final or definitive, there is in fact a dark side imposing the awareness that the unknown persists; or an indication of a point beyond, certain but unreachable; or the signs of an ancient death, skulls and bones as in Jung's dream, or sometimes a sarcophagus of a lost civilization. Particularly clear evidence of the symbolic character of existence is provided by these last places, where the irreducible presence of the unknown is revealed precisely in the perception of a mundane reality.

Finally it is possible to recognize, through these dreams, the *topoi* where the intersection of the unknown with the sensible is more inclined to reveal itself than elsewhere: in the first place death, which conjures up, perhaps more than any other reality, certainty and at the same time the unknown; then, as in the young woman's dream, the sexual focus; finally, the fascination of God, which takes the whole of reality towards the unknowable and makes the unknown the distant horizon and the ultimate foundation. These constants of existence reawaken the original anxiety through the separation in which they are generated, and at the same time the possibility of treating it, through the tendency to reunion inherent in them.

When, owing to the predominance and permanence of separation, that tendency breaks down, in other words when a splitting takes place, the anxiety that results is more often placated by cancelling out the very perception of doubleness, through denial or rejection of the separation. Then the essential difference of existence is forgotten, the inner relationship is lost and replaced by the illusory assimilation of one reality into the other. The Separator vanishes, or we aspire to dispel it, and believe that this is possible: the yearning for the ideal (which is not the joining of the two in the one, but the one without two, without difference, without separation and Separator) is born and the immanent sense, generated by this co-existence in difference, disappears.

It is Pothos who is sidetracked in that yearning, finding no rest in the forms of memory. But this means that he moves away from the reality for which he is destined, because he pursues, in order to pass from the lack of harmony of the present to the coming harmony, an ideal projected into the future, or an ideal that rises and judges. In this way, Pothos asserts a literal messianism, worldly or spiritual, individual or cultural—symbolized by words like growth, development, progress, upward motion, expansion, integration, totality, unity, completeness. The ideal is repositioned in this displacement of value from the present to a future goal, in order to make a denial that is still imperfect, the denial of the difference between the pre-existing and ancient reality of the soul, kept alive as memory, and worldly singularity.

That the domination of forgetfulness should persist and Pothos be deviated in the direction of the ideal and the future—releasing anxiety and guilt, depression and exaltation, rebellious and authoritarian violence—appears ubiquitous and necessary; so that our stories and our history are revealed as metaphors for an uncertain, obscure struggle, shown by partial maps, whose meaning is promised each time and precluded each time. In them, memory arises, persists, is lost, returns: the conjunction is transient, always exposed to the risk of separation, and yet possible.

In the redeeming image of the poet, the saint, the philosopher, of the 'great' man, which presents itself to us from every time and place, the *syn ballein* is personified in a lasting form, as a mediating daemon that takes care of the soul, since it succeeds in joining the two otherwise separate shores above the gulf. Venerating the memory of one of these men, as we have done here by evoking Jung through the thoughts, dreams and moments of his existence, we too, with him and through him, are able to recognize the symbolic destiny of our path and ourselves as generated by the soul.

CHAPTER TWO

In the Garden of Venus

Pothos, Roman copy after Skopas

In the storerooms of the archaeological museum in Florence is a statue of Pothos which provides us with an image of nostalgia. It represents a youth of ephebic appearance who is winged, stretches upright on crossed ankles, and lifts his right hand with the index finger pointing upwards. At his feet, a wild goose also turns its head upwards. The youth seems like a visitor to this earth, only recently alighted and already about to depart. His sojourn lasts just long enough to attract our attention and detach us from that world which we have believed until now was our only destination. He indicates a place elsewhere, reviving in our souls a memory which Lethe has not entirely annihilated.

The appearance of this winged youth alters our consciousness. What seemed like our own solid earth becomes a strange region, a land of exile. The seductive messenger has directed us back to the place where we were predestined to arrive but of which we are ignorant, forgetful. This home-land is revealed to us by the yearning flight of the youth who precedes us and draws us on towards a dwelling which is and has no 'where': whose material 'whereabouts' do not exist.

The original Pothos was sculpted by Skopas towards the middle of the 4th century, and much loved in antiquity. It has disappeared but numerous copies in marble and precious stones have been handed down. Pothos was not however originally intended to appear alone. Skopas had accompanied him with two other figures, Eros and Imeros, now lost, in a group which would represent the various aspects of love to anyone going up to the temple of Aphrodite at Megara. The particular relation Pothos then had with Aphrodite is evident in the wild goose which lies at his feet in all the copies and which we also discover in an antique vase of the 5th century, out-stretched in flight towards the heavens with Aphrodite on its back. It is in fact on the wings of Pothos that Aphrodite unites the two realms of sky and earth.

The sculptures at Megara find their original explanation, or at least the earliest one available to us, in a passage from Plato's *Cratylus* in which Socrates replies to Hermogenes' enquiry concerning the meaning of the words which indicate pleasure, sorrow and passion (*Cratylus* 419 b-420 a). When Socrates comes to talk of *imeros* and *pothos*, and sound their depths, he describes them as referring to the same reality differentiated only by fate. Desire (*imeros*) is a flux which envelops and impetuously drags along the soul it masters so that she craves for the present object: but if the object craved for is absent and far off, then the same feeling, called *imeros* when the object was present, is now called *pothos*, the desire which turns towards whatever is distant and cannot be reached. Socrates traces the origin of love, of *eros*, to the antique *esros*, that is to say that it 'flows in' from outside. While desire—whether it is *imeros* or *pothos*—streams from the soul towards the world outside, eros comes to her through the eyes when they are looking at the beautiful objects in which the flow originates.

There are already several classical instances of pothos in the pre-Socratic tradition: in the *Odyssey* first of all where pothos is really what motivates the characters, impelling them to travel and destroying them with the pain of waiting, as is the case for the swineherd Eumaeus, stricken with pothos for the faraway Odysseus, or Antikleia, Odysseus's mother, who is overwhelmed with pothos for her distant son and whose life is destroyed by the resulting torment (*Odyssey*, XIV, 144.) In Euripides' great tragedy, another victim of the Trojan war, Andromache, shows the same intensity of *pothos*, and speaks of *potho thanein*, dying of regret and nostalgia (*Andromache*, v.824). However, if we want to understand *pothos* in all the richness of its referentiality, and in particular as depicted by Skopas and those inspired by him, we must return to Plato and to that founding myth of the soul which he has Socrates describe in the *Phaedrus* (246 a-256 e). Here *pothos* is discovered in a connection with memory which is essential to it: 'let us give thanks to memory, for the love of which, and with nostalgia (*pothos*) for the beings of that time, this discourse exists' (*Phaedrus*, 250). Of what beings do ancient poems and tragedies conserve and represent the 'simulacra' (250 a), the visible appearances? And, similarly, what things in everyday life stimulate memory and nostalgia in the soul?

The answer is in the primordial myth which Plato narrates and which is also found in Sanskrit texts of the same period. The soul is a 'mysterious power' comparable to a 'union of powers in a team of winged steeds and their winged charioteer' (246 a). Whoever drives this chariot has charge of two horses, one of which is noble and good, and of good stock, while the other has the opposite character, and his stock is opposite.

Antonio Rossellino, The Chariot of Soul, 1459-66

Hence the task of one charioteer is difficult and troublesome' (246 b). The soul is a spirit, a 'mysterious power', as is evident from its wings, like Eros, who Plato, referring in the *Phaedrus* to an etymology different from the one suggested in the *Cratylus*, states is 'the God with wing (*pteron*) for his name' (252 c). The soul and Eros, winged spirits—and destined to bring together earth and sky—occupy together the 'in-between' (*metaxy*), and are themselves a *metaxy*, intermediate and intermediaries between the world of the senses and its metaphysical equivalent, bridging but also filling the gap.

The soul 'when it is perfect and winged…journeys on high and controls the whole world, but one that has shed its wings sinks down until it can fasten on something solid, and settling there it takes to itself an earthy body which seems by reason of the soul'd power to move itself' (246 c) Although similar to God, the human soul possesses in fact a native inferiority, the 'ignoble' horse, and a consequent lack of harmonious motion, as a result of which her wings may become detached and she will then remain exiled from her predestined habitat. However, the memory of the things she has seen when she was following in God's wake and was able to look heaven-ward, can be revived, although with difficulty, precisely in that multitude of sensations in which she is now immersed, because they can prompt the recollection of the time when the soul saw in its plenitude the reality of which this material world is only a copy and at that point, if only for an instant, the 'return' which nostalgia desires is brought about.

This winged soul, the soul-bird with its ecstatic flight, moves before us into the unplumbable depths of antiquity, towards the 'beginnings'; and at the same time is with us now, in a dream or fantasy. The man with the bird mask on the walls of Altamira and the man with a bird's head in the bas relief in the Lascaux cave are traces from the paleolithic era of the same fantasy, a rudimentary representation, perhaps, of a shamanistic ecstasy. Similar traces are found from East to West, and come to us from remote epochs as well as closer ones. On each occasion we recognize in them the conviction that it is possible for man to interrupt the continuity of this 'merely material' plane of existence, and experience a definite change of state which opens out towards regions otherwise unknown. Flight is provoked by a nostalgia to transcend the limits of the actual, into which one has fallen back as into a prison, and thereby effect a return to a condition of origin. The modality of the 'merely material' is transmuted, corporal heaviness disappears: in his winged ascent man recognizes his spiritual being and, realizing that where he now finds himself is his only true dwelling, establishes a firm base.

The spatial metaphors which indicate this mutation are however only properly apparent to the intuition of those who have experienced it. Its annunciation remains notional for those 'left behind' because they will understand it as a split between our world and a world beyond, both discontinuous in space and time, whereas it corresponds in fact to a shifting of the spirit which embraces change as a form of return and moves to another place, not within the space/time continuum. Some alchemists say that whoever is of the spirit and has the power to fly, to lift himself into the air, does not in fact need to move from this place into some other unknown one, because those only can fly who 'clothe the body in the habit of contemplation' (Coomaraswamy 1946, pp. 183-4). It is as if these people disappeared from our earth-bound sight when they have merely changed position, have 'emerged' into a realm which grants them an interior vision of this same world. We find veiled allusions to this phenomenon throughout the centuries, in Plotinus amongst others, towards the end of the *Enneads* (VI, 9, 69079).

The experience of flight is thus not foreign to us, however much our modern in-difference would seem to degrade and exile it to the margins of our culture, amongst dreams and imaginings. In those regions one can retrace its multifaceted nature, which, moreover, is not dissimilar from what Eliade has uncovered in relation to shamanistic flight (Eliade 1989). Although it would be possible to multiply examples, I want rather to dwell on one aspect of the phenomenon, one amongst many. In the dream I have in mind, the ability to fly surprises a man as he wakes. Emerging from sleep, he opens his eyes and performs those same movements he performs every morning except that this time they have the unexpected power of lifting him up into the air. Astonished, fearful, he would like to descend, but his body will not obey a will accustomed to experiencing as heavy what is now light and lodged above the ground. He then persuades himself to submit to the different features of this new body; he moves his arms as though he were swimming, as if the air had acquired the density of water; and these movements which are now like those of wings, allow him to travel around the room, to alight and to fly up once again. Fear gives way to a prudent enthusiasm. This flight of his seems to be without any practical aim, nor does it seem as if one will appear. It is simply that he can move his arms with elegant mastery and fly. When, in the days following the night of this dream, he turns his mind to his recent flight, he will feel—with a realism which brooks no denial—sensations in the joints of his arms which come from their having beat the air. This will be the equivalent of a definite experience, a skill from henceforth acquired.

However strange it might seem, a dream like this can be concealed for a long time and only narrated after a multitude of rehearsals and promptings. It is as though it needs to acquire an autonomous force, a force of persuasion, before it can be confessed; and at that point one will see the narrator smile with embarrassment, as if some secret were involved which makes him feel shy or of which he is perhaps ashamed.

That 'madness of love' which Plato discusses in the *Phaedrus* can also indicate a similar internal transformation: the feeling by which one is seized when confronted with appearances which are god-like (251 a). This is a madness not in itself damaging, but rather a 'gift of the gods, fraught with the highest bliss' (245 c). It is heralded by indications of a breaking free from the imprisoning confines of this material world in all its variety and diversity; indications provoked by those who, it is true, are still closed within these confines but in whom is revealed a manifest image of a God. A vision therefore of that 'Identity' where previously there was only Difference, the beloved appears like a God—a God in person—whom the lover consequently 'adores' and to whom he is prepared to 'sacrifice' (251 a).

Plato is not guilty of hyperbole in these affirmations; hyperbolic is rather what he describes: the action which launches us outwards, across the infinite and uncertain variety of Difference towards a Sameness which persists for ever. Plato in fact, following an archaic thought which we already find in Homer, represents the beloved in the guise of an *eidolon*, an apparition which retains the very life and soul of its divine model. A memorable figure expressing this relation occurs in the *Symposium* where Socrates is, in the words of his beloved Alcibiades, just like 'one of those little sileni that you see on the statuaries' stalls.... and when you open them down the middle there are little figures of the gods inside' (215 b)'.

That the beloved is seen by the lover as an eidolon allows us to understand why in the madness of love *pothos* is a daimonical, irreducible element. The *eidolon*, in fact, is the manifestation of a presence in this world which turns its head to measure the distance from its origin. This distance never diminishes because whatever in the *eidolon* makes itself visible and appears to us, in reality resides elsewhere. To encounter it for more than an instant is not given to man: it is something for which he can only feel nostalgia. If therefore we expected to embrace it as a thing of this world, then our arms would pass through it and impotently clasp our own bodies, as happened to Achilles with the *eidolon* of Patrolocus (*Iliad*, XXII, 100). Invisible and ungraspable by its very nature, whatever appears to us in such a way inhabits a dwelling which has no material existence: it irrupts into this world of the Many and opens a passage to *pothos* through which we escape. We are spurred and pricked on by desire, in a search which is endless and hopeless, because the *pothos* in question wanders within the confines of Difference, between boundaries both literal and illusory, when our true destiny is Identity.

Let us now turn to Plato and follow his description of the transformation which the lover undergoes from the moment 'a shudder runs through him': that immense fright equivalent to what the soul once experienced when, in following her God, she was able to rise above the clouds and glimpse, if only for a moment, true Being (*Phaedrus* 247 d). Whilst gazing on the beloved:

> First there come upon him a shuddering and a measure of that awe which the vision inspired, and then a reverence as at the sight of a god… and a strange sweating and fever seizes him. For by reason of the stream of beauty entering in through his eyes there comes a warmth, whereby his soul'd plumage is fostered, and with that warmth the roots of the wings are melted, which for long had been so hardened and closed up that nothing could grow; then as the nourishment is poured in, the stump of the wing swells and hastens to grow from the root over the whole substance of the soul, for aforetime the whole soul was furnished with wings. Meanwhile she throbs with ferment in every part, and even as a teething child feels an aching and pain in its gums when a tooth has just come through, so does the soul of him who is beginning to grow his wings feel a ferment and painful irritation. Wherefore as she gazes upon the [beloved's]beauty, she admits a flood of particles streaming therefrom—that is why we speak of a 'flood of passion'—whereby she is warmed and fostered; then has she respite from her anguish, and is filled with joy. But when she has been parted from [the beloved] and become parched, the openings of those outlets at which the wings are sprouting dry up likewise and are closed, so that the wing's germ is barred off. And behind its bars, together with the flood aforesaid, it throbs like a fevered pulse, and pricks at its proper outlet, and thereat the whole soul round about is stung and goaded into anguish; howbeit she remembers the beauty of her beloved and rejoices again. So between joy and anguish

> she is distraught at being in such a strange case, perplexed and frenzied; with madness upon her she can neither sleep by night nor keep still by day, but runs hither and thither, yearning for him in whom beauty dwells, if haply she may behold him (251 a- e).

Wounded by the madness of love, the soul thus turns towards its destined flight: an uncertain flight in the wake of the God she resembles and of whom the beloved is a mnemonic apparition. And it is Beauty which gives to this apparition a god-like quality because only Beauty is the perfect imitation of the divine (251 a).

The restitution of the soul to the God she resembles, this then is Beauty's mission. To her alone amongst the ideal beings is this privilege granted, to offer herself to our sight in a manifest way and thus to be worthy of immense love (250 d). Solitary trace of the One which manifests itself in the Many, Beauty seduces the soul; and man, brought back to life by its means, becomes also daimonical, mediatory, symbolic, as Socrates is said to be in the *Symposium*, because he himself becomes an *eidolon*, an intermediary between Sameness and Difference, the One and the Many.

Desire however becomes problematic because, although it certainly directs itself towards the material concreteness of the object, which is potentially available, it also seeks transcendence by contemplating what in the *eidolon* it would never be able to grasp. This is an archetypal problem which both proceeds and is responsible for each personal experience. Plato represents it as the erotic dialectic from which is derived the 'science of love' (*erotikon episteme* [*Symposium*, 210 e]): a science of the invisible archetypal model which we follow without knowing and by means of which we turn towards our God, where our destiny lies and where we have our being.

This science has taken its subsequent form in that love dialectic we call 'analysis'. And we call 'transference' the pathos which takes its ardent and uncertain flight in the wake of this God, as Jung has been able to show (Jung 1946c). A flight in which one continually urges on the other; and where it would be difficult in fact to distinguish the beloved from the loved or establish who captivates whom, taken up as both are in a circular flux of desire. This is because between the two appears Anteros, reciprocated love. Then:

> ...that flowing stream which Zeus, as the lover of Ganymede, called the 'flood of passion', pours in upon the lover. And part of it is absorbed within him, but when he

> can contain no more the rest flows away outside him, and as a breath of wind or an echo, rebounding from a smooth hard surface, goes back to its place of origin, even so the stream of beauty turns back and re-enters the eyes of the fair beloved. And so by the natural channel it reaches his soul and gives it fresh vigor, watering the roots of the wings and quickening them to growth, whereby the soul of the beloved, in its turn, is filled with love (255 c).

Just like the lover a short time ago, so now also does the loved soul contemplate herself 'as in a mirror' (255 d); analogously in fact to the way both contemplate that same god whose followers they are.

Whatever inclines towards the 'return' manifests itself initially in descent, as a search for the One amongst the Many, as the Gnostics imagined it or Jung in *VII Sermones ad Mortuos* (Jung 1925a). And analytical psychology has described these phenomena no differently in calling them 'projection', 'transference' and 'assimilation'. The apparition, the *eidolon*, is descended from God: there where he was previously is now the place which attracts our attention.

Discord between her two horses therefore arises in the soul: one of them intent only on a materiality to which it would like to reduce the apparition so as to subject it to its will whilst for the other, as for the charioteer, when it glimpses 'the beloved flashing upon them ... its memory goes back to that form of beauty, and he sees her once again enthroned by the side of temperance upon her holy seat (254 b). But when an effort is made to grasp hold of the image then it withdraws, vanishes and leaves only a de-animated object in its stead.

When in the sixth chapter of the first book of the *Enneads* Plotinus plunges further into his meditation upon Beauty, he evokes, in order better to explore the furthest limits of this problem, the myth of Narcissus with results that will then be garnered by the Neo-Platonists who followed him. Whoever flings himself on these simulacra, he says, in the hope of making contact with reality, is like a man who wants to seize hold of his own beautiful image drifting on top of the wave, one who immerses himself in the current, and disappears. It is not the contemplation of the image in the mirror, conserved there by its reflection in the world of the Many, nor the loving imitation which ensues from that, but rather the pretension to eradicate the image's difference—literalism (that is)—which, impeding the 'return', encloses him in a sepulchre of Narcissian fluid.

This is the danger due to the longing of the first horse, which does not however constitute merely an impediment since, while both its companion and the charioteer are gravely agitated, this animal at least carries them all into the neighbourhood of the beloved (254 a). Desire and inhibition together therefore, and only together, greet the *eidolon* because they correspond to its own heterogeneous nature.

Every follower of a god, all those who are 'faithful in love', seek from trace to trace his effigy (252 e) and, according to the nature of their deity, look for a soul expressive of that nature (253 b). Nostalgia torments them as well as an anxiety which derives from the compulsion 'to fix their gaze upon him, and reaching out after him in memory they are possessed by him, and from him they take their ways and manners of life, in so far as a man can partake of a god. But all of this...they attribute to the beloved' (253 a).

It is for this reason they urge the beloved to 'walk in the way of their god' in order to make his soul as like him as possible (253 b). This *mimesis* is thus an ethical code and presupposes dramatic transformations which from the beginning announce themselves with a violent shudder, with terror; and in the problematics of desire. A *mimesis* contrary to the usual processes of imitation whose similar features belong to the rule of Diversity, whereas this intimate, interior modelling of the Self on God appertains to the rule of Similitude where love seems to possess the power of modelling men on the things they love.

What Plato called Beauty and has such seductive force is thus the manifestation of an interior essence by virtue of which things become *eidola*, apparitions. Plato states that not only people but all visible things harbour this essence (250 e, 251 a). It is a late Neo-Platonist, Proclus, who peered further into the matter and was rewarded for his pains by the recognition of subtle invisible links between things: links between both them and their different gods because Beauty manifests herself to everyone by different means and in different ways. Proclus recognized that the same essence appears in a diversity of beings and imagined that each 'apparent' being was linked by a 'sympathy', a reciprocal and simultaneous attraction, to its 'celestial principle', its 'angel'; and that these angels formed a choir which accompanied the God at their head (Corbin 1969). Centuries after Plato had described the myth of the soul in the *Phaedrus* this late, distinguished follower revived without damaging it. While Plato seemed to conceive the relation between man and his God in the progressive coming together of one with the other — in so far as man can share in God's nature, Proclus, who nevertheless is in accord with his great predecessor, signals, and everywhere recognizes, the traces of above all an inner *pathos* which is the very foundation of the relation: not only manifest in things themselves but also in the God. He recognized a pervasive *sympatheia,* a compassion, binding all things in affinity to each other and to God: a nostalgia evident in that 'tropism' (as he called it) which irresistibly attracts things into a reciprocal closeness, a necessary intimacy—within a complex constellation of images. The *mimesis* of which Plato had spoken in the *Phaedrus* is then fulfilled, Proclus makes us understand, in a surrender of the soul to the *pathos* which controls her, which she shares with God, and which makes her like him: a process in which they are many mediating factors to which the soul's motions are linked.

These discrete entities, which join in sympathy with and in the soul, these things which she reflects and in which she recognizes herself as in a mirror, are also the images with which we live surrounded and in whose multiple affinities resides that God who touchingly calls on us to follow him. A 'transitive' passion which traverses the soul, God and all things and leads them towards a 'becoming other' which is in fact a becoming like: a move towards a community of essence; and as we recognize that our steps are guided, our original physiognomy transformed and our gestures moulded, we discover a more exact rhythm which is always the same and yet always other. It is in this *mimesis,* this return through compassion, that Proclus discovers the profundity of beings, their interior essence—the unique possibility mortals have of breaking through into the Invisible. This is the experience to which Jung refers, in his most rigorous epistemological paper, when he insists on the need for analytical psychology to abolish itself as a science because every explanation of a vital psychic reality cannot be anything other than that reality itself (Jung 1954b,2). Here he is echoing that cognitive function of sympathetic *mimesis,* the return of the soul towards her God, which Proclus had been able to recognize; and positing that condition of stasis, standing still, which is the *episteme* of analytic psychology.

The transformation—of which Jung also speaks several times and especially in the text to which I have referred—is thus induced by sympathy, day after day, gently. Yet in this compact fabric sometimes occurs a lacerating eruption, that 'shudder' or 'immense fright' Plato spoke of whereby the thread is lost, as lost as the previous personal identity; and if this amazing violence eludes our attention we have little understanding of the catastrophe this represents.

Henry Corbin helps us here with his accounts of the percussive violence of Love in those *Persian Tales* of its faithful followers, comparing those stories to others very close to us Tuscans, tales by Dante and his Circle in the first instance, and then Petrarch. The experience of Beauty is not, he says, straightforwardly pleasurable or joyful: what in fact we are used to calling an aesthetic experience. It is much more and rather a *tremendum*, an event which inspires fear and this because 'the bound towards the object also surpasses it' (Corbin 1976, p.211). The transparency or sudden apparition of Beauty is certainly manifest as an *eidolon* but not known immediately as such; because that recognition — Corbin reminds us — occurs only when it is realized by the lover what Beauty implies: 'the conspiracy of the spiritual with the sensuous' (Corbin 1976, p.211). Until this happens, the eruption tends to reveal and thus painfully accentuate Difference. The wound, which this *tremendum* opens in the soul, has in fact a disturbing power of alienation, which the 'melancholy of love', witnessed to by centuries of literature, makes clear.

This metaphor of a 'wound' has quite rightly become traditional, indicating as it does a narrow passage through which one penetrates violently in search of secret, protected place; because the advent of Love opens a gap, widens a fault. There is thus a scission in the experience of reality, sometimes to the point where its basis is questioned and judgement is turned upside down. What then is truly 'real'? This world which seems a prison from which our only option is escape; or that other domain which figures as an already sampled promise of a garden of delights? A garden however where permanence is doubtful and to which access might well be forbidden: access to the 'true' reality from which the lover might sometimes be exiled forever, without hope and this is what melancholy amounts to in the end. The euphemisms and banalities into which we fall when we interpret the experience of love are thus like veils which attenuate the overwhelming power of the apparition; they are a method of isolating what brings us shame because such is the effect of the *tremendum* which results from direct contact. Suhrawardî is aware of this when he describes, in the *Vademecum for Faithful Lovers*, Zolaykha's meeting with the young Joseph:

> When she saw him, Zolaykha wanted to come forward, but her heart's foot stumbled on the threshold from amazement and vertigo; she moved beyond the confines of what could be sustained: challenged the power of limits; she ripped from herself the protective veil of reasonable behaviour and sank at once into the domain of melancholy (Suhrawardî 1976, p.312).

Inaugurating long ago an interpretative tradition which reaches up to Leon Robin and beyond, Hermias read the *Pheadrus* in the light of the *Timaeus* and believed he recognized in the two horses which pull the soul's chariot, the image of the Many. As a dyad or in multiplicity, unequal or dissimilar, the Many reveals itself as a principle awkward to manage, hostile to the One which attempts to keep it within bounds. In the *Timaeus* (46 d, 47 d ff, 69 d) the Many is identified as that principle of Necessity which brings about whatever lacks harmony; is in fact Necessity, as a principle of disorder, the 'random cause' which provokes the fall of the soul from the cortege of its God (or rather it is the lack of harmony amongst the horses which provokes it, as the *Phaedrus* makes plain). As far as the soul is concerned therefore the two horses would be the Many which pre-exists what we know as life, and the charioteer himself the One—he who is perhaps possessed of transcendent vision.

The soul is thus a daimon who inhabits 'the immense emptiness which separates the two worlds' (*Symposium* 202 e), participating in both and thereby connecting them, at once eternal and mortal. One might say of it what Diotima said of daimons or spirits to Socrates: 'Divinity, you see, has no direct contact with human kind; only through the intermediary of daimons does it relate to us; all its dealings with men, in sleep or in waking life, are transmitted through them' (203 a). By way of these daimons—images, complexes—God's will reaches and is imposed on man, whether or not he is aware of it, and he is brought close to a God as to his own destiny. Prayer, the due which man pays to whoever controls him at such moments, is also made possible by the intervention of daimons (202 e). The soul is the site of this activity, and the *eidolon* therefore of Difference.

From this inner union in the soul between the One and the Many is born Eros, as the *Symposium* explains (203 b-204 c). His father is Poros—'Resource' or 'Plenty'—a manifestation of the eternal, but a drunken one. In the presence of the Gods, during the banquet for the birth of Aphrodite, he becomes inebriated, falls asleep and then forgets; and in the period of forgetfulness he couples with Misery, in whom there is nothing of the eternal but only the material, and who has not even been invited to the banquet. Yet Poros himself was a guest: godlike although with a relation to the divine which is unstable.

This fundamental duality of the soul, chained to the material by her passions but occasionally drunk with memories of the eternal, widens the abyss of human melancholy, that immense void which separates two worlds. Man is a powerless spectator of his own history, as he experiences both an intoxicating and transitory exaltation, which nevertheless fails to free him from the despised inferiority of the material world, in all its impenetrable opacity, and a dull despair, arrogant and envious denier of any possible contact with the divine. However, in the very depths of this melancholy, in the forgetfulness of the Gods and when, with Misery on the alert, there is emptiness and inferiority, the impulse for union unexpectedly arises: Eros is born. A 'stinging gadfly' is Plotinus's name for this Eros in the fifth chapter of the third *Ennead*:

> ...even if it obtains what it wants, there it is again empty-handed! Nothing ever satisfies it ... since only what is properly comprised in its own nature can be truly satisfied; but the essential indigence of Eros leaves him forever wanting more and even in those moments when he finds himself abundantly supplied, he has no means of keeping what he has (III, 5, 64).

Eros traverses the 'immense void' which divides the human soul and which, though he may briefly close the gap, always yawns wide once more; and he thus provides mortals with both intoxicating riches and misery, at one and the same time.

Hesiod describes how, with the blade of his sickle, Cronos divided sky and earth into two: and how, amputating the sky's genitals, he sanctioned the irreversibility of the separation and of the gap which ensued: a gap as apparent in the world at large as in the souls assigned to mortals (*Theogony*, 178-193). However, everywhere on earth remained traces of the sky, because, from the amputated genitals which Cronos had thrown into the sea, derive whatever recalls for man the now distant Uranian world, and conserves the possibility of intimacy. From the sea's foam, eddying round the sky's genitals, was born the divine Aphrodite, and this very foam from which she derives her name (aphros: *Cratylus* 406c) suggests her value: the light presence of air, of the sky, infusing the heaviness of water and earth. This is the mythical event which Plato echoes when in the *Phaedrus* he affirms of divine reality: 'to Beauty alone was granted the immense privilege of being clearly visible and worthy of immense love' (250 d).

The birth of Aphrodite reveals the intimate connection the young Goddess has with old Cronos, their affiliations with the same constellation of myths; and an old tradition which runs from Renaissance Neo-Platonism to the most recent studies of archetypal psychology, recognizes in human melancholy a way in which the two gods converge.

Let us then pick up the Cronos theme. It is said in the *Cratylus* that the word from which his name is derived, *coros*, 'expresses the fullness and pure nature of the mind' (396 b); whilst the neo-Platonists saw in the action of his sickle the fragmentation of the supreme One which thus falls into the Many from which Aphrodite then emerges. This is the sense in which Pico will understand it in his *Commentary on a love-song*. For him, the genitals of Uranus infuse the *prima materia*, which is otherwise amorphous, with the seed of ideal forms: 'because ideas would not have in themselves variety and diversity if they were not mixed with formless nature, and because without variety there cannot be beauty, so it justly follows that Venus could not be born if the testicles of Uranus did not fall into the waters of the sea' (Pico della Mirandola, *Commento*, II, xviii ff; Wind 1967, p. 133).

Proclus, in his *Commentary on Plato's Cratylus* recognizes Cronos as 'the originator and benefactor of intuitive things' and notes the homophone with 'Chrono', or Time (*Orfici* 1968, p.58). This similarity of names, and thus of the essence of which each is a sign, seems to be the result of a progressive assimilation of the two gods which are identified as one as early as Plutarch (Panofsky 1962). Neither is this similarity difficult to understand in that it is Cronos—'the pure nature of the mind', the 'father of all things intuitive'—who separates, establishing difference and form where previously there was formlessness, and thus allows the emergence of those discrete entities through which the world is made apparent and by consequence the progression of time. The blade of Cronos's sickle is the dawning manifestation of time; an intuition which distinguishes form and thus binds together time and beauty (*Enneads* III, 5, 25).

In a passage of the *Timaeus*, Plato says: 'Now the nature of the ideal being was everlasting, but to bestow the attributes of its fullness upon a creature was impossible. Wherefore he resolved to have a moving image of eternity, and when he set in order the heavens, he made this image eternal but moving according to number, while eternity itself rests in unity, and this image we call time' (37 d). Plotinus could be said to broach this topic from the point of view of Aphrodite, the soul of the world, when he writes: 'now there comes into play a power without peace, the soul, yearning to transform into diversity the vision of what lies above and not content with what had previously been presented monolithically' (*Enneads* III, 7,

102). The creation of a material world in the likeness of the eternal thus proceeds by fragmentation; but before anything else the soul herself becomes part of time, imposing temporal sequence on what was timeless: *in fact time is the very life of the soul which passes 'eternally from one state to another'* (III, 7, 108). 'With her first step the soul stumbles into the essence of time and makes it at one with herself' (III, 7, 138). This would therefore be that 'eternal image, moving according to number' because 'it presents itself in life bit by bit, separately, burdened with time, and this ulterior "always" of life carries always with it an ulterior moment; and all previously lived life is also laden with past time' (III, 7, 107). Only in this way, Plotinus tells us, can time 'purchase from hour to hour its rights of citizenship in the heart of Being and thus within these limits we can imitate the eternal' (III, 7, 111). This is the eternity manifested in Aphrodite, in the appearance and disappearance of everything; and aesthetic intuition discerns precisely this manifestation, or rather an intermediate soul which mediates between time and eternity.

The personal emblem of Lorenzo di Pierfrancesco de' Medici, who commissioned Botticelli's *Birth of Venus* and *Spring*, was a medal showing a serpent, curved in on itself so that it formed a circle, an ancient image of eternity.

Medal of Lorenzo di Pierfrancesco de' Medici, verso

The serpent is not however biting its own tail; its head, resting on the ground, remains outside the circle of eternal perfection thereby indicating the fall of the soul. Studying the medal, we become intensely fascinated by this circle: although 'fallen' the serpent remains in the sky from which it derives, uninterruptedly. Like the Neo-Platonists who preceded them, Ficino and Pico also signaled this possibility and it is not surprising to find an image of it in the emblem of a man for whom Botticelli painted the two Venuses, images of the *anima mundi* which inspired the Renaissance.

When Botticelli began the two works destined for Lorenzo di Pierfrancesco de' Medici, he meant to resume in images the complete vision which Florentine Neo-Platonism had of Aphrodite, of which Edgar Wind has given a full and sensitive reconstruction in *Pagan Mysteries in the Renaissance* (1967). Here it is worth noting that the painting which Vasari entitled *Spring* was rather meant to represent Love's metamorphoses as they are manifested in the Garden of Venus; and in fact the many flowers in this garden make us pause and demand our attentive consideration.

Sandro Botticelli, Primavera, 1478

The flowers are a common presence in both paintings even if their purpose is different. In the *Birth of Venus*, the naked Goddess is about to be veiled with the figure of Spring throwing over her in fact a flowered mantle to cloak her nudity. In the other picture the flowers spread to cover the little garden from the moment of the metamorphosis of Chloris who, before being enveloped in the passionate breath of Zepherus, is of a single colour. The inert, opaque Chloris and the naked Aphrodite, visions of Beauty, are the extremes between which intervenes—in order to join them together—the flowered mantle which both veils and reveals. Indeed, in the flowers multiplicity and Beauty discover their simple and recognizable connection: the Beauty which is given to mortals as an indication of diversity, that which reveals itself in the fragmentation of time; the veil which both displays and conceals, a plurality of polychrome images.

There is something however in this garden painted by Botticelli which becomes comprehensible only after an attentive look at the details; and evades the notice, on the other hand, of whoever relies on a vision and interpretation of the ensemble. It evades him because he is concentrating on what is functional for his interpretation or for the general aesthetic outcome. I mean the flowers: these particular flowers which Botticelli has chosen to paint one by one, faithful to the actual features of each one and to the way in which it actually appears. Forty-one different varieties of flowers (Levi D'Ancona 1983).

Sandro Botticelli, The Birth of Venus, 1478

In this attention to the multiplicity and diversity of things, we can recognize a lesson by Botticelli which perhaps derives from the apparition before him of Aphrodite. It is in this aesthetic intuition of particularity that Aphrodite is born again; the rest is an interesting allegory from which moreover the Goddess might well be absent.

This 'precise lyricism', as Botticelli's imaginative pictorial style has been called, is relevant to analysis because it represents one of its exemplary modes. The garden of Venus, where the metamorphoses of Love take place, is in fact where analysis resides: a garden in which we can, like Botticelli, identify the flowers, one by one, contemplating, smelling and delicately touching them—the great stream of flowers which flows out from the passion of Zepherus and Chloris. Analysis understood in this way consists in the discernment of the imaginal world in which the coming into being of a single existence, in all its beauty and transience, takes place; and in a correspondence with the compassion which pervades that world.

When Aphrodite governs analysis together with Cronos, there is an opportunity for the flowering of *multi flores*, the varied and diverse physiognomies of reality, to which words give substance. The elements which make up the atmosphere in which the exchanges take place are noise, lights, objects, the presence of the other; bodily sensations; emotions; and then the memory of people, objects and environments in which the person speaking lives and has lived; and the people, things, places, atmospheres experienced in dreams; fantasies as they are remembered or apparent now; all these elements which seize hold of the patient or appear before him as if they were in a picture or on the stage. These are the distinctive individual presences whose manifestation language permits, the small, varied flowers which we can tend in the garden of analysis. When we turn our attention to these minute appearances—and without suddenly distancing ourselves in order to dominate them, as happens when concrete and particular appearances are immediately reduced to abstract interpretations—then we hear their gentle murmur and there grows in us the feeling of intimacy with a whole world; a feeling which lives with us as a presence in our own ambience or as *umbrae* emerging from those depths we call 'inner'. Aesthetic intuition always discerns a singular reality, a distinct event, an alterity unless it is inhibited by the monism of the dominate consciousness and there prevails that static assimilation and obscuring of difference which gives rise to our omnivorous isolation. Now however appear those things to which we pay careful attention: they appear and disappear, autonomously, without being forced to arrive or clung on to as they fade away. They are witnesses of the eternal image, 'moving according to number' and the means by which we are inducted into a particular cosmos.

But attention cannot be forced, merely sometimes given; because the things which the soul reflects, which appear and disappear and return unexpectedly, are distinctive for everyone: they are that which allows them to share the *sympatheia* of a God. Because only if a God wants to draw us towards his likeness can we become aware of these realities which then become truly present: an event whose arrival is signalled by nostalgia and compassion, both of which prepare us for this free and sympathetic intimacy. We can perhaps call to them but only then to find ourselves waiting because the subject and arbiter is no longer 'I' but that God who time after time directs through images our desire or excites our fear, and in a manner which conforms with the world for which we are destined.

Intimacy with this reality, of which a comforting reflection remains in the heart, then gives rise to *mimesis*, the slow accommodation with a God, in so far as man is permitted to participate in God; and thus the discovery of form—soul—and sense. We can call this process of imagining 'cosmological' because it introduces us, slowly, into the different worlds of images which belong to us and from which we are as it were exiled. This process is not however a 'construction in analysis', rather a fragment traversed by various narrative threads, multiple but coexistent; it does not give rise to an identity but to its unmaking, which is what the word 'analysis' indicates,—an unraveling of the pre-existing texture, a dissolution, a loosening of the bonds which also symbolises death. The analysis is thus not built up; rather it destroys that which had stiffened in order to survive and submits it to time. The eternal flux of Aion, the 'true Essence', is then revealed in the appearance and disappearance of each image, in its return and its departure, forgotten: this is Kairos, the fugitive moment, another offspring of Cronos, the aspect of time in which its reality is constituted and meets that parcel of eternity granted to mortals. Here is another winged daimon, deaf to human intentions and yet, with its forelock waiting to be seized, offering a momentary succour.

The conjunction of Aphrodite and Cronos in analysis arouses an aesthetic attention and confers sanctity on the present moment; and in that present moment they are actualised symbolically and in conjunction. The dance of the three youths of Megara: Pothos, Imeros and Eros, in front of Aphrodite's temple, is the harmony which ushers in the Goddess: the desire which moves towards individual realities, the nostalgia for that which gleams in the distance, and also a love which it is both engendered and received. It perhaps echoes the Botticellian dance of the three Graces, Chastity, Voluptuousness and Beauty, in the garden of Venus, where three youths initiate the action: Zepherus, ardent with desire; Eros of the flaming arrow, and a pensive Mercury who with his caduceus nudges aside the clouds and peeps through, the outsider, *pothi*, hermeneutically nostalgic. A dance which in the garden of analysis is constituted in the *kairos*, and in the *pietas* which allows it to emerge; while the soul takes its form, 'bit by bit', as a world of images.

CHAPTER THREE

The Imaginal Action

We find active imagination right at the outset of Jung's research, when it took on form and significance in his dialogue with Toni Wolff, and then went on to constitute the very foundation of the work that followed. From then on active imagination, even when it appeared to have vanished in practice, has in fact been a decisive and distinguishing presence in the Jungian tradition, an implicit form-thought which has radically conditioned the accessibility of Jungian expression itself and the appreciation of its hermeneutic potentialities. I would like to go back to the teaching that continues to stem from it and pick out a number of aspects, in order to emphasize and gain a better understanding of a question I consider decisive: that of the imaginal ego, of the inactivation it undergoes and its return to action.

In particular, what interests me here is a technical prescription, one which defines active imagination and distinguishes it from the passive experience of imagination. For this we can turn to the formulation that Jung gave it later on:

> ... if you recognize your own involvement you yourself must enter into the process with your personal reactions, just as if you were one of the fantasy figures, or rather, as if the

> drama being enacted before your eyes were real. It is a psychic fact that this fantasy is happening and it is as real as you – as a psychic entity –are real. If this crucial operation is not carried out, all the changes are left to the flow of images, and you yourself remain unchanged (Jung 1963, par. 753).

This prescription, apparently so simple, actually turns out to be hard to put into effect; to such an extent that in general it is only when the analysis reaches a considerable depth that active imagination becomes practicable for the patient and begins to produce results. In fact the existence of such a constant difficulty leads us to think that there may be some injury at its origin, which has to some extent dissociated the ego from the anima, or has made their possible links disturbing.

To understand the terms of the question, it is necessary to bear in mind a condition that is preliminary to the intervention in the imaginative process. This entails assuming an attitude of conscious expectancy towards the psychic event, i.e. one that excludes, at the outset, any wish to interfere: an attentive interest that implies respect and concern for what is being addressed, and abstinence from any use of the emerging fantasies, in order to avoid the transposition of feelings and images into objective reality, or rather the transformation of the imagined occurrence into it.

It is to such an attitude that the realization of images is entrusted, i.e. making them accessible to perception as 'another', distinct from the subject who is paying attention. In other words, the images usually take shape very slowly, and it is the interest in them that allows them to reveal themselves fully, and their drama to emerge. It is attention that permits the revealing of their difference from the subject, who up until that moment was in a state resembling that of pregnancy.

Abstinent interest performs the function of demarcating the threshold that separates two potentially different realities, which only in this way can truly be defined and placed in relationship: images, in particular, come to express a value of their own and, in the persistence of the difference, a power of attraction and influence, without assimilation. Such an interest is the means by which the ego is set free in that moment from its one-sided connections with objective reality and introduced *as well* into that imaginal reality, of which it is now able to discover the substance, the value and the demand for engagement. The ego that comes onto the stage of images, which enters into their drama, is the only one that has the responsibility to intervene in them: precisely because it is now there and part of the imaginal scene. Only in this way can communication between the characters of the drama be set in motion; then the intervention will not be arbitrary, but suggested by the complexity of the drama, and so consistent with its internal reality.

The experience that is attained by this means is the experience of the imaginal world, and in particular of the ego as a content of the imaginal. In this sense we can speak of an 'imaginal ego', just as we speak of a 'dream ego', which is in fact just another name for the same thing, i.e. that aspect of the ego complex that takes part in imaginal reality.

This differentiation of the ego complex, whether it is made manifest in the course of an active imagination or, on an everyday level, as 'dream ego', is not an artifact. It is its structural necessity, and the necessity of its presence and its action is revealed by its function, by what seems to be its specific task: keeping the ego complex connected with the different aspects of mental reality, i.e. of reality in so far as it is mental. It is precisely the recognition of this function that explains why its presence has difficulty in making itself felt over the course of an analysis. In fact it can be assumed that the defence against psychic suffering entails a variable degree of inactivation of the imaginal ego; and disturbances of psychic integration would be a consequence of this. Indeed the purpose of the inactivation of the imaginal ego is to anesthetize the effects of those troubling psychic situations which only the imaginal ego, by participating in them, can integrate into the complex of the ego.

The consideration that in analysis the imaginal ego only emerges little by little also throws a peculiar light on the relationship between analyst and patient. In fact the analysis can be regarded as an event, and at the same time as imagination of this event, in other words as the crucible that permits a life to be turned into an account, a story. At the start of the analysis there is a sense of asymmetry between analyst and patient as far their capacity of opening up to psychic reality is concerned. The analyst finds himself almost alone in putting into effect, as if in an active imagination of his own, the prescription of an attentive and abstinent interest in what takes place during the session: a reflection that turns every event, whether recounted or immediate, into an imagination, and every interpretation into a way of recognizing that psychic events have a reality of their own, different from the objective one. As a result, the imaginal ego, which in the patient appears to be dissociated from the ego complex, will be able to find its own projective representation in the analyst: this opens up the possibilities offered by every projection, of introducing an otherwise unconscious psychic reality onto the scene, and of arriving at a subsequent, differentiated expression of it. In order to attain such an expression, the analyst must not fail to pay attention to those signs in the patient that reveal progress in his or her empathic relationship with the images of the anima; a recognition that will have all the more weight if it is accompanied by that of the concretisations, of the imaginal gaps into which the analyst also falls.

In fact this awareness can attenuate any identification with the imaginal ego on the analyst's part – favoured by the conception of analysis as a workshop of images and of the analyst as a maker of images, a hermetic condition that brings with it the risk of this kind of inflation – and trigger in the patient the reintegration of the imaginal ego as a function of the ego complex. A process that leads to the opening of psychic space and permits imaginal action in its various moments; and in particular makes it possible to discern the configurations of transference, and thus fosters an emancipation from the innate compulsions to transference.

I would now like to recall, through two dreams, the conduct of an analysis in which I feel that several fundamental aspects of this process can be recognized.

In the first dream the patient, a man of thirty-eight, found himself in the city of his birth, in the streets he had known as a child; and the sister whose hand he was holding was still a little girl. These streets were filled with hostile groups representing conflicting ideologies, which pushed them here and there, so that his little sister was almost suffocated. Walking through the streets he came to an unfamiliar square, in which stood a church that was partially sunken below ground, and could be reached by going down a few steps. A ritual was being performed in the circular basement of the church: the priest raised a large white Host in the air, attracting the gaze of the whole congregation, who then came up to receive pieces of it. Among them he saw his sister and his own companion, who gave him a humble and tender look, waiting for his permission to receive communion. Touched, he felt the sense of superiority he had toward the congregation fade, gave his consent and went up to receive a fragment of that single Host with her. There was a hiatus. Then, as if awakening from a long sleep, or emerging from an unconscious state, he heard the voices of his companions calling him. He realized that he had sunk into a prayer with no images or words, into an undifferentiated state from which he surfaced slowly and with difficulty, with a different awareness of himself. They were alone, he and the unknown companions who were calling out to him, lost without him. As he listened to this appeal, he felt a sense of compassion for them grow in him, and with the compassion came the decision to seek with them the goal they shared. He knew he would lose forever the state of communion he had just rediscovered, and chose to sacrifice it out of compassion.

In another dream, the same night, he and his companion watched with amazement as his little son began to sing at the top of his voice.

This account, given with intense emotion and wonder, has led me to think, over the course of time, that the ego had found that central place, deeper and until then unknown, where its action became ritual, or imaginal, because it became the actor of a complex metaphorical transposition. From this centre of the anima the ego emerged with a different consciousness of itself, of its responsibility toward other psychic personas: no longer just torn apart by conflicting passions, and unaware of an integrating function whose action was blocked, but capable now of an empathic insight into different emotional states. The imaginal ego seemed finally to have succeeded, in this story, in differentiating itself from other psychic personas, and at the same time to have entered into a true and dynamic relationship with them – which started out from a sharing of pathos, from a compassion that created connections and a common orientation in the space of the anima.

While this may have been the outcome of the process, we should not ignore the fact that it was fostered and sustained by the emotional intimacy with the women who had looked at the man with trust and love: the little sister of the past, encountered on the streets of memory, and the companion of the present, or perhaps the Anima. And it may also have been the smile on the analyst's face, which appeared to him in a dream he had a month later.

In the dream the patient went to see his analyst, meeting him in a farmyard. They started to talk. The analyst's face was all smiles. There was a growing feeling of warmth between them, as if an affection previously held in check had been allowed to emerge. The things around them were steeped in sunlight and their shapes were clearly visible; especially the road, whose contours the patient could feel distinctly with his feet. The two of them walked together for a while and then said good-bye, slowly and sadly.

The imaginal ego seemed to have been set free, and the patient began to truly inhabit his dreams and the space of analysis:

with a hitherto unknown participation, discernment and trust – as he also started to really inhabit the world of daily life, in which he now found, unlike in the past, soul and beauty as well as sorrow. It also seemed as if the imaginal ego no longer coincided, in projection, with the analyst; on the contrary, that it had separated from him and was beginning to become a stable and independent reality, the prelude to another separation that it was now possible to foresee: the end of the analysis.

CHAPTER FOUR

Towards a Living Reality

The pictures that Morandi began to paint as he turned thirty showed things steeped in a subdued, dim light, or in semi-darkness: on the point of yielding up the mystery of their presence to the light, and at the same time about to withdraw, to vanish, dissolved in the shadow that consumed them from the inside. These were my thoughts, standing in front of a still-life from those months on display at the Pinacoteca di Brera.

Giorgio Morandi, Still Life, 1920

And it seemed to me that the forms struggled to make themselves visible, and that this hesitancy filled them with a sense of unease. It was as if the imminent possibility of their disappearance revealed another presence, one that transformed the visible from a quiet manifestation of everyday objects into the portent of an unknown, perhaps unknowable life.

If the invisible were not to appear in the visible—Morandi seemed to be saying—not only his pictures, but painting itself would be nothing but an empty shell, a fraud. And in fact Morandi did not represent anything, least of all the objects on which his and our gaze fell, which for this reason were chosen from among the most ordinary and humble of things: it was not this his aim, but to seek the lost essence of painting, its power to cherish the otherwise invisible remainder of the imagery of our transient world. The more humble the image and reserved the artist, the greater the exaltation of this fundamental sense of painting. This religious devotion, which turned each of his pictures into an icon, made Morandi particularly appealing to me. For he had taken on the extreme responsibility of curing painting of its ontological disorientation in order to bring it back to its essence. His art was a Neoplatonic *epistrophe*, a memory that harked back to its archetype, to its original meaning, the act of painting.

In his presentation of those pictures in Florence in 1922, de Chirico described the young painter's work in a passage that is still worth reading today:

> He looks at a group of objects on a table with the emotion that stirred the heart of the traveller in ancient Greece when he gazed at woods and valleys and mountains thought to be the abode of beautiful and surprising deities.
>
> He looks with the eyes of a man who believes and the inner skeleton of those things which are dead for us, because they are motionless, appears to him in its most comforting aspect: in its most eternal aspect.
>
> In this way he participates in the great lyricism created by the last, profound European art: the metaphysics of the most ordinary objects. Of those objects which habit has made so familiar to us that, however wise we may be to the mysteries of appearances, we often look at with the eye of someone who sees and does not know.

It was not for nothing that Heraclitus of Ephesus claimed nature to be full of daemons' (Briganti and Coen 1984, p.21).

These words of de Chirico's were very penetrating, identifying a crucial place—and a crux—on which the meditation on 'reality' of some of the masters of the 20th century was converging. This is evident if we reread a classic passage from Jung's *Psychological Types*, a work published in those same years:

> Living reality is the product neither of the actual objective behavior of things nor of the formulated idea exclusively, but rather of the combination of both in the living psychological process, through *esse in anima*. Only through the specific vital activity of the psyche does the sense-perception attain that intensity and the idea that effective force, which are the two indispensable constituents of living reality. The autonomous activity of the psyche, which can be explained neither as a reflex action to sensory stimuli nor as the executive organ of eternal ideas, is like every vital process, a continually creative act. The psyche creates reality every day. The only expression I can use for this activity is fantasy. (Jung 1921, pars. 77-8)

From Jung to Morandi, and right up to our own day, the task of healing modern humanity of its loss of soul—which is a loss of the imaginal sense—and of the consequent loss of 'living reality' has seemed decisive to many; and this with the recognition that the world is pervaded by soul, and thus permits the deep echo of things in the human soul. If it has been said of Jung that he was more of a poet than a scientist, and if even a psychoanalyst can regard a painter as his teacher, this is because their work has its roots in the same region, the one that Hillman has called the 'poetic basis of mind' (1983, p.14) and that Jung, following Goethe, identified with the realm of the Mothers, the realm of Mnemosyne—the now repressed imaginal memory—and of her daughters the Muses, cloaked in 'the images of all creatures' (Goethe 1976, II v.6289). It seems necessary to go back there, in order to restore to life a world stripped of its many daemons: a world reduced to inanimate things, no longer recognized in the forms of the imagination, but only in those forms that make it available for unlimited use.

It is a dramatic and uncertain return, for it entails the erosion of that monism of the consciousness which constrains the complexity of living reality within an unequivocal conception, so that the subject can make it available. A loss of intimacy with reality of which Morandi too spoke, as Francesco Arcangeli recalls: 'When Morandi says that "today people no longer see", he puts his finger on one of the fundamental manifestations of a great crisis in life, thought and custom' (Arcangeli 1981, p.167). And Morandi went on to say: 'I believe what we see to be the creation, the invention of the artist, if he is capable of tearing down the barriers, that is to say the conventional images that get between him and things' (Magnani 1982, p.34). So it is the imagination that for Morandi, as for Jung, 'creates reality day-by-day' and makes a gift of it. And to respond to the call of reality we always find an expression, whether we follow Jung or Morandi, of the need to give up the monistic ideal of consciousness. A change that in Hillman's view can even be catastrophic, because more often than not 'only this weakening or "falling apart" breaks through self-enclosed subjectivity and restores it to its depth in soul, allowing soul to reappear in the world of things' (Hillman 1983, pp.31-32). An initiatory violence that the alchemists called *mortificatio*, the frequently painful disintegration of those 'conventional images' (Morandi), of those 'literalisms' (Hillman), that is needed to free the soul from being caged in an inert material, and thus to enter a 'living reality'.

This process can take place in different ways, and I began to recognize and study it frequenting the studio of Carlo Mattioli. Spontaneously revealed there was a mode of procedure from which I could reconstruct, with the aid of the artist's sparing words, the process by which his works were generated—and how they had been generated over the years, right up to his most recent manner.

It was possible to recognize a constant stylistic feature, a process of reduction which in Mattioli signified 'eliding, stripping away, paring to the bone, identifying with a few simple structures', as Pier Carlo Santini put it, going on to say:

> Without hurry, without anxiety, without impatience, Mattioli allows his projects to mature over periods of meditation that may be very long, although he can also be dazzled by sudden visions. I think that the reduction of the image to its essentials—perhaps the most constant feature and aspect of his work—is prepared over the course of this detachment from objectivity, which entails forgetting about morphologies and paying less attention to direct and immediate suggestions and impressions. Hence the process—and by this I mean the

> formative process—is radically pruned and deeply rooted in the inner being. The "duration" and substance of Mattioli's expression are ensured by this intense process of maceration aimed at synthesis (Santini 1984, p.15).

Carlo Mattioli, Rose Nude, 1962

A process of this kind appears to be in line with the 'metaphorical perspective' of which Hillman speaks, going along with the action of the soul, which operates by 'transposing the meaning and releasing inner, buried significance', and which, while it 'brings about the death of naïve realism, naturalism and literal understanding' (Hillman 1983, p.30) i.e. of every vision that is exclusively instrumental or that does not go beyond conventional forms, prepares for the advent of an unconditioned opening up to living reality instead.

In Santini's passage referring to Mattioli's imagination, as well as in this one of Hillman's, there are words whose deeper resonances need to be heard: for 'dazzling visions', 'innermost, buried sense' and 'maceration' are not rhetorical exaggerations but events.

Like the ancients, and like de Chirico and Morandi, Mattioli sometimes saw daemons in the forms of nature. And it was a dazzling vision, for Beauty is revealed in the moment, as it is only in the moment that we encounter the eternal in time. It also awakened Eros, which was then bound to that apparition. That particular reality, that particular way that being has of making itself present in an event, now rends the veil of conventional knowledge and, emerging from concealment, becomes entirely visible. The living reality of the thing is there, precisely in the form in which it appears: it is the soul of the thing that is unveiled in the moment. But it is only slowly that the image becomes stable and is made accessible to reflection: after 'reminiscence'—the power of the soul to restore time to the eternal—has steeped, in its absence, the residual veil of the conventional and subjective context. An image that has at last become a form of the soul, a now independent living being which has within itself a lasting potential for expression.

Mattioli tried to interpret the image by working rapidly and with intense concentration; tackling the same subject from one picture to another, but varying it each time, in search of a focus that was never conclusive. With the result that a single image came to be represented in a cycle of variations, each corresponding to it but none of them exhaustive, even though complete in itself. Each representation preserved, in the immediacy of its execution, the immediacy of a vision now stripped of further determinations: something original, primary. In fact the image painted by Mattioli was stabilized in that in-between where matter begins to congeal into a form, and the absolute light within the matter passes through in a distinct irradiation: here the particular appearances persist, and at the same time are transfigured into imaginal reality, and thus we are introduced to the vision of a world pervaded by soul, to the only reality that can appear truly 'real', living, the one that the imagination presents ordered into a cosmos.

As remote from expressionistic pathos as he was from impressionistic description (both of which exalt the subject who 'feels' or 'sees'), Mattioli was a poet of the cosmic event, of what 'comes from' the cosmos. In his works it is evident that the being has its most complete form of apparition in the soul, in the opening where human being and world encounter one another, where things and gods meet, and out of which a cosmos comes into existence. There is the hearth where unease finds rest, the place for which we can be homesick in our exile. For, as Hölderlin put it in one of his poems, 'man dwells poetically on this earth' (Hölderlin 1966, p.372).

Carlo Mattioli, Beach in Summer, 1972

CHAPTER FIVE

Life Inside Death

There are artists whose images can reveal obscure places of the soul, especially places where necessary but evasive truths are hidden. A fine example is Zoran Music, whose most significant history begins in a concentration camp, at Dachau. 'It was there where I found my truth'—he explained in an interview. ' Before the deportation I didn't have any personality, I allowed myself to be influenced by this or that. . .' (*Music* 1992, p. 212).

He had been deported to Dachau at the age of thirty-five, because of his friendship and suspected collaboration with members of the Nazi resistance movement. He stayed a year, until the liberation of the camp. A number of statements, made in diverse circumstances many years later, and some drawings, forty in all, remain as a testimony to that period of his life. In his accounts he mentions himself only rarely, once to say that he had not suffered physical violence, and another time when he remembered drawing. He describes the landscape of horror, the life of the lager shared with the others, in a sober style which we can also recognise in the drawings, done furtively, with chance materials, and then hidden wherever possible:

> They are still today with me the eyes of the dying that, like hundreds of pungent scintillae, followed me whilst I cleared a way, striding over them. Shining eyes that in silence asked help of one who could still walk.... Towards the evening those who were dying, and among them also those only believed dead were heaped up like pieces of wood on a pile, as for a pyre, almost a turret. A hallucinating turret that moved, that one could almost have said creaked, if these creaks hadn't been the last groans. During the night the snow fell lightly—it was in March—the morning after, the turret no longer moved.... I lived in a daily landscape of dead, of dying in apathetic expectation.... The corpses were piled everywhere. At noon, soup. Holding his mess tin, the still standing skeleton looks around for a place to consume his broth. He finds a free place on the head of a corpse—and drinks the liquid which, if not thick, is at least hot. He doesn't even think where he is seated and where he places his small piece of bread, made from sawdust and potatoes.... When you wake up you count the dead around you. One... two... three... above... below... next to you (*Music* 1995, pp. 232-33).

In Music's accounts, his hints at the life of the camp, at violence, terror, remain in the background, like passages necessary to the narration; instead the dying, the dead are in the focus of his memory. He had drawn them then, in the camp; he returned to depicting them after 1970, for five consecutive years and almost exclusively them, and again in 1987.

During those early years of the 1970s, when he was immersed in the recalling of them, he had a dream:

> I was in the middle of a playing field. All the stands were filled by corpses sitting next to one another, the whole arena full of dead. It wasn't sad; indeed it seemed a great treasure for my work. Unexpectedly, as if by enchantment, all the seats, as if mounted on wheels, slid and disappeared from the field together with the corpses. I awoke suddenly, terrorised by having lost my treasure (Peppiatt 2000, p. 16).

What I have said up to now, and what I will say below, is only meant to be a meditation on this dream, a meditation that includes the work of Music, which can be seen in relation to this dream even when it precedes it chronologically, as if dream and work had the same matrix in the soul. I could not risk more, even if the subject takes me close to 'Auschwitz'; because as far as that place is concerned, for us, only silence is possible, apart from horror.

At Dachau, Music had begun to draw during the last weeks before the Liberation, when surveillance had just begun to slacken:

> Timidly I begin to draw; perhaps thus I save myself. In danger I would perhaps have a reason to resist. The first attempt, hidden in the drawer of my lathe. Things seen on the road heading towards the factory: the arrival of a transport lorry: an open stock truck: the dead falling out.... Later I draw in the camp. The days pass... Soon I am seized by an incredible frenzy to draw.... I draw as if in a trance, I am morbidly attached to these pieces of paper. I was as if dazzled by the hallucinatory grandeur of these fields of corpses. Seen from a distance, they seemed like the patches of white snow, silvery on the mountains, like the white spots of flocks of gulls resting in a lagoon against the dark background of a storm out at sea.
>
> Whilst drawing I clung to a thousand details. How much tragic elegance in these fragile bodies. The details so precise. These hands, the thin fingers, the feet, the mouths open in the last attempt lo breathe some air. The bones covered by white skin, almost pale blue.
>
> How much zeal not to betray these subtle forms, to succeed in almost exclusive rendering them as precious as I saw them, reduced to the essential.
>
> I was as if gripped by a febrile state, seized by an irresistible necessity to draw so that this grandiose and tragic beauty would not escape me. I lived each day for itself only—tomorrow would be too late. For me, life and death depended on these sheets....
>
> After the visions of corpses, stripped of all the exterior requisites, of all superfluities, deprived of the mask of hypocrisy, of the distinctions with which men and society cover themselves—I believe to have discovered the truth, to have understood the truth—the terrible and tragic truth that was given to me to touch (*Music* 1995, p. 233-34).

Of these drawings, Music succeeded in saving, at great risk, only some, which he kept to himself for a long time. The majority—thirty-four sheets—were shown at a drawings exhibition at the

Centro Pompidou in 1988. In only three of them are the living recognisable, but even in those, there are also the dead or dying; in all the other drawings they are the only presence.

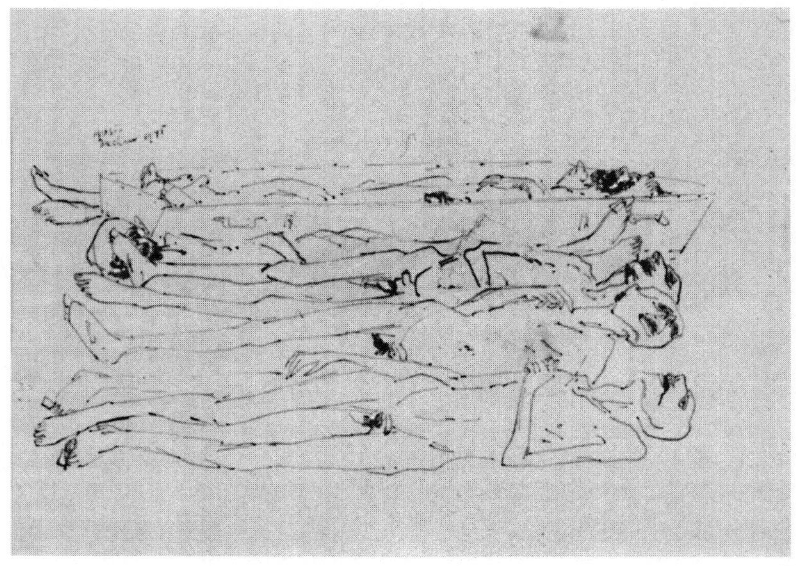

Dachau, 1945

It was therefore the 'hallucinating grandeur' of the fields of corpses, the 'grandiose and tragic beauty' of those bodies reduced to the essential that attracted the young painter, whose own body was not dissimilar to those already dead, but yet alive, whose consciousness was drawn into a state of identity with the event. That just that event became, at least in memory, an experience of truth and beauty, as if to disclose a form of being, leaves us astonished and thoughtful, confronted by an abyss of meaning. Music also said: 'After Dachau something broke inside me. Before I had many certainties: suddenly I lost them, and I understood that around us there is only emptiness' (*Music* 1992, p. 212). A desperate expression in appearance only, because where truth and beauty are recognised despair is relative; it accompanies the dispersal of what in that event has been destroyed; the previous vision of the world, an ideal construction.

In conjunction with this subject I would like to present, as a counter-point to the images of Dachau preserved by Music, an account of the hanging of three prisoners at Auschwitz, among them a child. We read of it in Elie Wiesel's *The Night:*

The three victims mounted together on to the chairs.

The three necks were placed at the same moment within the nooses.

'Long live liberty!' cried the two adults.

But the child was silent.

'Where is the Good God? Where is he?' someone behind me asked.

At a sign from the head of the camp, the three chairs tipped over.

Total silence throughout the camp. On the horizon, the sun was setting.

'Bare your heads!' yelled the head of the camp. His voice was raucous. We were weeping.

'Cover your heads!'

Then the march past began. The two adults were no longer alive. Their tongues hung swollen, blue-tinged. But the third rope was still moving; being so light, the child was still alive ...

For more than half an hour he stayed there, struggling between life and death, dying in slow agony under our eyes. And we had to look him full in the face. He was still alive when I passed in front of him. His tongue was still red, his eyes not yet glazed.

Behind me, I heard the same man asking: 'Where is God now?'

And I heard a voice within me answer him:

'Where is he? Here He is—He is hanging here, on this gallows...' (Wiesel 1981, pp. 76-77).

The Event that we call 'Auschwitz' marked, perhaps, for the monotheistic consciousness to which we belong, the beginning of an eclipse, the obscuring of the image of a God, creator of good and of evil, as some passages of the Torah testify (*Amos* 3, 6; *Isaiah* 45, 7), who by means of good and evil provides mysteriously for man's history. This loss leaves a painful vacuum in which, as Hans Jonas maintains, a new conception of God would begin to take shape, which that Jewish philosopher attempted to define in a Platonic mode, narrating the myth of a suffering God who has renounced omnipotence (Jonas 1987). A new conception, but also similar to others, arose in the past at the margins of the prevailing culture, traces of which have remained, as omens that we can perhaps now gather and understand; also because today analogous metaphors are recognisable in the arts, in literature and—most interesting for us—in the analytic experience, where it is possible to consider them as expressions of the Self. They impose themselves as such by their position in the history of an individual, and for their function in it; surprising and wounding our expectations, dissolving our subjective goals and our theoretical models. Indeed, in the light of such images, the concept that interprets the autonomous action of the Self in the same way as a divine action, creative and providential, that integrates and guides towards wholeness—a central metaphor for the second-generation Jungians—seems merely an ideal construction.

Music's works and testimony help us to approach these emerging images, and to attempt to make sense of them. When in 1970, Music began to paint the dying and the dead of Dachau, he gave the same title to every painting: *We are not the last.* At Dachau, he recounts, they used to say 'We are the last.' This title, precisely because it negates the latter affirmation, separates the extreme images to which he refers—images of death but also of truth and beauty—from chronological succession, from history, that is from the occasional, and acknowledges in them a manifestation of the eternal: as Wiesel's child is eternal. In this way a foundation is recognised where every foundation seemed to have been destroyed, where the most deep-seated weakness reveals itself. In other words, it is not so much a question of the absence of a foundation, but rather the possibility of imagining it not as a positive nucleus that generates and constructs, but rather as a 'black hole', an active emptiness that attracts and dissolves every ideal identity.

How does the soul respond to violence, to offence, to abuse that humiliates it, to pain that breaks it? This question is so serious, and the answer so difficult, that it has always remained at the centre of psychoanalytic reflection. If imagination is indeed the life of the soul, the means by which the soul flows in the world and by which the world becomes soul, what happens to imagination following a trauma, and how does it respond, if it responds, to the trauma? And why and when is a trauma really a trauma?

Precisely because imagination *is* the life of the soul, it is soul itself, as Jung has taught us; thus the wound involves imagination and the trauma can also annihilate imagination. Imagination prepares, if it can, an answer, assimilating what happened in order to transform it into an event of soul, a comprehensible experience, an epiphany of meaning, a myth; thus imagination transforms what has happened from a state of disturbing estrangement to a psycho-poetic process.

The offense is often obscure: most intense, intolerable to the point of incomprehensibility, it leaves no apparent traces. Or it is an irreducible glare that remains like an implacable wound in the memory. Or it is almost imperceptible but extended in time, masked and variously interpreted, and even justified. In each case, its extreme consequence is that petrifying Medusa's head: a petrifaction of the imaginal Ego, whose mediating function between the emotive material and the ego complex is thus impeded, in a defensive attempt that is itself destructive. When this happens, the emotive material may remain isolated, remote from the ego complex; isolated from the soul, the traumatic event is kept at a distance like a mere fact, irreducible; isolated from both, it lacks a form, presenting itself instead as a lacuna.

The imaginal Ego's surviving strength transforms the *prima materia*—the emotional material generated in trauma—and accompanies the memory's autonomous action, which slowly assimilates the traumatic event in its mythical form and thereby reveals its ultimate meaning for the soul. This is why Music felt that, at Dachau, to draw was a question of life or death. Not because he was a painter, or to preserve a testimony, but so that the imaginal Ego could begin to differentiate a form in the 'hallucinating' visions, in the upsetting and otherwise intolerable reality that day after day overwhelmed him with its boundless power and absorbed him in its ultra-human dimension; a form for the inconceivable and otherwise unsustainable paradox of horror and beauty. In that way, for Music Dachau began to become an event of soul, his internal 'treasure'. By now old, and almost by way of comment on the dream that I noted earlier, he was able to say serenely: 'I hope that this vision of death remains always in my unconscious' (*Music* 1992, p.212).

After the Liberation, Music settled in Venice, began to paint, and met Ida, the companion with whom he lived until his death.

Post Dachau, how to look at the luminous world that surrounded him, how to surrender himself to the sweet memories of his childhood, and above all, how to fashion them into painted images? Adorno said that after Auschwitz, poetry is no longer possible: but this is the affirmation of someone who lived the years of horror in a tranquil university *campus*, not of someone who survived a death camp, like Music. The years between 1946 and 1952 were among the most felicitous for his work. Images of the lagoon were the first to appear, then the hills of childhood traversed by herds of horses, ferries carrying oxen, Sienese and Umbrian landscapes, small female nudes and, like Byzantine icons, numerous portraits, of himself and Ida.

How do these works help us to understand more fully the workings of the imaginal Ego?

Dachau had taught Music to observe from his own solitude, and to dwell on essential things. In this renunciation of appearances, ideals, expectations, and thus the subject's excessive power, things become ensouled. An empty space, a distance, is opened, and within this space, which is an interior space, images come, not looked for, and not dominated by the ego complex. There is something of the antique in his paintings of those years, Music describes them as 'oriental', 'Byzantine', like the historical roots of his soul. They are distant images, not approachable; separated from whoever looks at them by a space that makes them appear to be from a different time; from infancy, but from an infancy of the soul, with its non-reducible wonder. A slow but continuous rhythm passes through them, interweaves them, a melody skims over them, light, subdued. Everything flows away, but at the same time, everything remains. Memory is the faculty of love, it gives back to eternity that which time devours and hate destroys. It does not prevent the loss, does not obstruct death; that is not in its power, nor is it in the power of love. Memory is a mode of compassion.

What relationship does Dachau have with all of this, with having 'understood that around us there is only the void?' Why so much sweetness, even though melancholic?

Here the dream of a man who, like Music, was a little over thirty-five years old and whose history was, naturally, quite different, is helpful. In it, a man, closed in a small room, perhaps a cell, was writing a chronicle of an event about which all mankind was aware and anxiously awaiting the outcome. While the man wrote about it, the dreamer was present, monitoring the facts, while listening to their narration: a cosmonaut was flying in his cockpit, searching, on behalf of all men, for a life that would fill the skies. His face, now visible, was distorted by an expression of infinite sorrow, and was coloured by a changing light, ranging from livid white to purple. The story of the man now became like a sorrowful song; it related that the cosmonaut had not found any life in the skies, that a void surrounded the earth, and that mankind was alone. The two men then embraced each other in tears. They now realised that the only thing that they could do was to care for the fragile, unique life that existed on the earth; nothing could give life back to destroyed life. The dreamer woke up sobbing, feeling himself to be not only the man who recounted the story and the cosmonaut, but also one of expectant mankind. The cosmonaut's face reminded him of the colours of a solar eclipse, at which he was present during his first melancholic break-down, the black sun of his soul. He began to think that what he had then discovered with terror, and had later attempted to flee, to mask—his weakness, the fear of living—was rather his truth, part of his way of being in the world, and thus it wasn't necessary to follow a 'high' self-ideal in order to defend himself. On the contrary, the breakdown had returned him to his true way. The dream represented the end of an inflation of the spirit and of an isolation, the descent into the fragile everyday world from the desert of the skies, in which until then he had exiled himself.

To recognize the void that surrounds us seems to have this power—when sorrow is not suppressed and the heart can understand—to approach with *pietas* the simple life that is given to us, and when it is lost, to love it in memory.

> Music's story also teaches something else, that the achievement of a elevated moment of interior concentration, with an intense bond to the images of the soul, is in any case precarious. Invited to exhibit in Paris, Music moved there in 1952, entering a cultural climate which, in many respects, was alien to him. He began to frequent the painters' circles, then completely dominated by abstraction. Music, who did not paint 'abstracts', began to doubt himself, to believe that he 'was wrong': 'I felt small, weak, without strength. Surrounded by these giant personalities of painting and by the critics, prepossessing arbiters who controlled the general trend, I felt useless to myself and I was almost embarrassed to show my *Small Horses that pass by...*, I felt exiled from the world' (*Music* 1995, p. 237).

Yielding to this strong pressure, he tried to conform; or rather, he returned to that subtle self-hate that he had experienced before Dachau, which impels us to search among powerful external images for the models in which to annihilate ourselves. He then began to violate his figures, stylising them, reducing them into apparently abstract forms: this continued for years. His new work was favourably received, and was finally awarded the international prize for graphic art at the 1956 Venice Biennale.

These were years 'punctuated by the greatest solitude...': an internal isolation that was caused by the closure to the Self, and that therefore couldn't be broken by visits from the intelligentsia or the acknowledgements of collectors and museums; and even less by making a painting that preserved only a distant echo of his imagination. It mattered little that an interior formal coherence was perhaps recognizable in those paintings, because images are different from a style; they are not stylistic conventions but living beings. They demand devotion to the particular form in which they are put forward, for which they are uniquely recognisable and reach a perfected existence. Indeed, if we remember that these autonomous images are 'soul', that they are in fact its most particular expression, it becomes possible to understand that the abandonment of this devotion leads, as a consequence, to an interior split, sometimes even a true schism.

We must remain aware of this thesis, for it will be confirmed by the subsequent unfolding of our story. At Dachau Music reconstructs his truth, which the Parisian experience causes him to lose again; a consideration that enables us to reflect upon the subjective value of 'traumas', which is variable because relative to the Self's point of view, which is never the same. Indeed, from the perspective of the Self, something can appear to be a loss that otherwise might be judged a gain or a success; and vice versa.

This state of loss continued not only during the 1950s, but in a more attenuated way also during the 1960s, amidst uncertainties and anxieties. Then, in 1970, Music found a way to return to his *interior* Dachau, allowing himself to be reached by the images of the dead and dying, and with them, by his 'truth'.

He drew, etched, and painted *We are not the last* for five years, concentrating almost exclusively on this theme.

In the images of those years, every descriptive realistic residue, which we still find in the Dachau drawings, has disappeared. The figures are immersed in an absolute space, a dark shadow which contains the bodies: the one and the others emerge, reduced to essentials, from a canvas or paper remaining partially untouched. As is the case with images of memory or of the depths of the soul, the forms emerge in the fight with the unformed, they exist in a precarious equilibrium. Their regression into the indistinct, their disappearance, appears imminent: they exist, but at the same time they don't exist; they are not of this world, and yet they are. There are no individual physiognomies; there is no longer anything of the personal, not even pain, humiliation, fear. There is the same hunger for air, the last attempt to hold life; the same reversed genitals, like felled trees; and hands, rigid in an uncompleted gesture, which no longer grasp anything. This is man. There are no executioners; there are no survivors, because only the dead and the dying are in the place of truth. Light emanates from their faces, from the bodies; there is no other source, no *elsewhere* that illuminates. A delicate blossoming of colours, just perceptible, sometimes interwoven with browns, with whites; a silent joy, veiled, accompanies compassion. The place of truth is also a place of love.

We are not the Last, 1970

What Music said about the value Dachau had for him goes back to these years and these images. It was the product of an awareness that perhaps was not so clear during the years following the Liberation, having rather matured by torturous roads and in the pain of bewilderments, like a light that blooms in the night of the spirit. It is precisely this, the awareness of the Self that unmasks the imagery in which, from time to time, the Ego identifies itself, and produces a spontaneous divestment, the fall of a decidua that had seemed to be a stable structure. As a result, the world and events are seen in a different way.

Jung asserted that an obscure, unconscious impulse governs the configurations of consciousness and strives to find form; or rather that the Ego is the field of the formative action of the Self, which tends to adapt it to its own shape. But after Auschwitz, the Self no longer seems to be composed of images like the *Anthropos,* which Jung originally recognized and studied. The images that now emerge remind us, instead, of the *Ecce homo,* of this anonymous man of Music's who is unknown and unconscious, without a crown of thorns, with the Shadow that crowns and defines him; the new images remind us of Wiesel's child, in whom an impotent God was manifested. This seems to be the centre of gravity, or the void, that attracts consciousness with a gleam of truth: every other image of man is undone by it, like a mirage, a deceit.

It was not easy for Music to separate himself from the images that had absorbed him for five years. Indeed, only in 1977 did he succeed in finding others intense enough to constitute a metaphor that would transpose the bodies of Dachau into new shapes; the rock masses that over the centuries had detached themselves from the sides of the Sella and gathered around its slopes.

Rocky Landscape F, 1979

He went to draw among those rocks, allowed their presence to reanimate living images in himself, which had perhaps always been there. As he explained:

> In reality, what is before me is not something new; it is similar, if not identical, to what I carry with me, which has always been with me, perhaps from infancy, but which, every so often, fades, threatens to leave; and in that moment I need a new impulse, support, a new 'way of seeing', in order to allow it to re-emerge, new and strengthened.
>
> Thus—looking—the time passes, also the hours, and I begin to live this nature, and it seems to me to be part of this universe. Slowly, everything begins to move around me. In this silence many things, perhaps small, perhaps unimportant, begin to move.... Thus I stay there, seated on a stone, immobile, and everything gradually becomes alive: a porcupine ventures to come out from a thicket, two marmots pet each other on the rock opposite, a lark that sang, rising towards the sky, hurls itself vertically and lands on the stone nearby, and the butterfly that clings to the pencil does not want to leave. The time passes and I have the impression of seeing myself as in a mirror in this landscape; it sends me back my voice, and my drawing is like the echo of what I have projected upon these rocks. This life is important for me. All moves in silence, I even seem to hear the grass grow and I don't even realize that I have allowed myself to dream (*Music* 1995, pp. 238-39).

The silence, the immobility of death, continues in these stones, which, however, shelter the movements of a minimal life, they are the necessary scene of it. The divestment makes us attentive to what was earlier unnoticed, that lived without existing for consciousness. The subject no longer fills the space, it has retreated, it has become more subtle, and allows the other to live, it contemplates its quiet presence. Now, the centre of consciousness is at a point where it seems that every subject disappears: the painted images emerge from a void that keeps them distant, separate, surrounded by a spellbound silence, interwoven with a tenuous light, with an intensity that is completely interior.

The *Rocky Landscapes* were followed by images of Venice seen beyond the water of the canals—that of *The Giudecca Canal* and *The Tip of the Dogana*—also devoid of human presences. Then, in 1983, his gaze began to linger along the narrow streets, on the houses, on the walls consumed by salt, on the windows and arcades, where it surprised the men who passed in silence. In that period Music painted the intimate solitudes of *Venetian Houses*, and together with them an interior, the *Atelier*, with the painter at his easel on one side, and the seated model, his companion Ida, on the other. Separating them, but also uniting them, is a large space in which the two are immersed, a profound emptiness vibrating with suffused low light, an absence that supports and gives meaning to the man and woman.

Atelier, 1983

In this emptiness, and in its silence, one experiences the anticipation of an event, or rather an advent, the arrival of images. The *Interiors of Cathedrals,* done in the following year, display a metamorphosis of this motif: the light radiating from the rose window illuminates the empty interior space like a gentle glance that tenuously lights the forms which, by its action, slowly emerge from the darkness.

Cathedral, 1984

In *Ateliers* and *Interiors of Cathedrals* Music had achieved a perfect representation of imaginal consciousness, and seemed to have found the centre of his soul, the place 'without place' from which to view the world. Thus it was; but yet again not in a stable mode. A restless, uncertain period began for him: he no longer succeeded in painting essential images.

This time he did not remain in a state of crisis for long; he knew where to find the source of his 'truth': he returned to his *interior* Dachau. In 1987, by which time he was seventy-eight years old, he returned to paint *We are not the last,* and continued to do so for the whole year . In this way, the *Self-portraits* and the portraits of *Ida* that he had begun to paint in the preceding years and the fundamental motif of the painter with his model, the *Atelier,* found an analogical way to transform themselves.

Indeed, in 1988 he began a new cycle of paintings; in these his entire interest was concentrated on the human figure, but only on those figures which he could imagine to know 'from inside', as he once said: himself and his wife. Then, from 1991—and these are the last known canvases—the personal references disappear, the female figures disappear: we see only slender, trembling, solitary masculine figures, the nude bodies of a *Man* who washes himself, of an *Anchorite* who meditates, or the dark shadow, barely visible, of a *Wayfarer.* The dead of Dachau are now present in these other extreme images, in the faces themselves, in the bodies, as if they were destined to this outcome; not because an old man is already a dying man, but because of the same fulfilment of a destiny, that is to 'conform' to those dying ones, to the truth that they announce.

The similarity of forms between the images of *We are not the last* and these establishes a continuity of meaning. Perhaps certain subtleties have been lost, the language has become skeletal, yet more essential, but the images are formed in the same light, are outlined against the same darkness, emerge from the same desert. The postures, gestures, are still those of every day, the faces maintain the changing vibrations of the emotions; and yet, it is as if the distance between a *here* of life and a *there* of death, preserved until now by virtue of a differentiated language, could now lessen and disappear.

In order to understand this process, we cannot ignore the occurrence of one of the most painful events for a painter, weakening eyesight, which seems to have deprived Music of almost all but his interior gaze. Having thus lost the strongest link with exterior things, with the lights of the world, his painting now becomes, in the most immediate sense, the reflected image of the soul; or better, as he himself said, the way in which the soul sees him.

I would like to conclude this meditation with three of his most recent works, *Self-portrait as Aristotle, Wayfarer* and *Man.* The first and second of these are similar to two works by Diego Velazquez, respectively *Aesop* and *Menippus,* in the Prado; the third, to a self-portrait by Pierre Bonnard entitled *The Boxer.* In an artist, historic memory is never casual, and when an artist is mature and old it reveals not only the profound affinities, but also the invisible *lari* and the *penati* towards which the artist now turns at the end of his work; because it is towards them, after the long journey, that he searches for his rest. We must understand that for a painter the imaginal world takes the form of painting, the archetypal images appear in that shape, and the return movement from personal to archetypal assumes the same form. Thus Music could say, in a colloquium, that his self-portrait represents 'a Music tormented by painting, because only painting could torment him. It is all that he loves and that makes him live in doubt'. The images of painting are images of the soul, they constitute the soul that loves him and torments him.

Self-portrait, 1988

Self-portrait as Aristotele, 1989

Aesop and Menippus were considered, in Velazquez's time, representatives of classical wisdom. Aesop's fables, especially, seemed to contain all the wisdom necessary for living; they were the very voice of the Wise Old Man. But not for Velazquez, who fashioned an Aesop and a Menippus who were uncertain, anxious and in pain, attempting in vain to preserve their antique prestige. The dream of wisdom has failed; the 'wise man' is, in reality, a weak man with a wrinkled disheveled face, who arouses, if anything, pity. Aristotle points to the earth with his finger, as we see him in Raphael's fresco. We have no wisdom that guides us, not even the wisdom of the unconscious; we can live day after day like errant tramps, and look at reality with a detached benevolence. This is what Velazquez and Music seem to say. And the heroism of the contender, of Bonnard's boxer, is only a gesture that reveals instead his foolish desire, the weakness from which it is born and to which it relapses. There is an infinite, tender humility in this self-portrait of Bonnard, where he shows himself, as in the other self-portraits, from a mirror, not as a presence in the world, but as a reflection of the soul. Bonnard's self-portraits are among the images in which the man of today can best recognise his own truth; perhaps because of this, Music evokes *The Boxer* in a painting where he depicts his own old body, and which is called simply *Man.*

Man, 1991

Wisdom, strength, these constitute a dream of the Ego, perhaps a necessary dream. The task of the Ego, which cannot be eluded, seems in fact to be the one of building identities, possibly strong identities, which enables self-orientation in the world, in the affects, with the conviction of certainty. Doubt, torment, these constitute a gift of the Self, which no longer appears as the *omnipotent Anthropos* to whom one reaches in order to emulate, or as the omniscient Wise Old Man to search out and listen to, but rather as a weak child, a foolish old man, a victim, a dying man; as a void, a nothingness, that erodes from within every structure of the Ego and pulls it towards its final destiny: death. Traumas, defeats, humiliations, decline, every experience that diminishes, empties, limits or leaves us abandoned, is assimilated in this obscure depth. An increase in destructive power accrues to it, but also the possibility to be transmuted into a form in which the Self manifests itself and acts; just as the insistent return to the wound can become the way the soul has of getting and keeping it 'in focus' in order to make it a home of the Self, a place of transformation and a centre.

What does the Self concede in exchange, what does it allow to enter the field of the Ego, to substitute there the illusion of strength and wisdom, through the split that failure holds opened? One response is suggested by a dream of a man who is nearly sixty years old. In it, a woman, perhaps a cloistered nun, saw, beyond the grille that separated her from the interior of a church, an unknown man, wounded, suffering, abandoned on the nave pavement. Within her, compassion was ignited like a light, strong enough to dissolve the grille and propel her towards the man. While she raised him in her arms, the church itself disappeared. The woman felt as if she had been enveloped, contained, and with her the man who dreamed, and with both of them the suffering man, enveloped and contained by the light of compassion.

CHAPTER SIX

In the Interregnum

On a warm spring morning, I was looking at one of the frescoes that Fra Angelico painted in the cells of San Marco, in Florence. Leaning on the door jamb of the first cell, I saw a small window opening onto the roofs and sky, and on its left the *Noli me tangere,* Mary Magdalene's meeting with Christ in the guise of a gardener, in the garden that stretched in front of the open and empty tomb. I asked myself, perplexed, why it was that Angelico had painted the fresco right next to the window, and thus with the light coming from behind; and why in that cell, the first of many, he had chosen to represent one of the last events recounted in the Gospels.

I knew that nothing, in those days, was left to chance. And so, if I was going to understand, I would need to do some patient interpretation. The significance of that placement, I thought, could only lie in the use to which the cell was put, as an enclosed space in which a monk made his home. But how could that sense be construed in such a way that all the phenomena involved would, as far as possible, be covered by the interpretation?

The window opened onto the world and onto the changing weather, onto the variegated aspects of the manifold. On the other hand the painting, precisely by presenting itself as an analogue of the nearby window, underlined its dissimilarity, for it offered a vision not of the appearances of the world, but of the mystery that is cloaked by those appearances: a reality outside time and space, eternal, at last made visible in figures that resemble what forever remains the same. In this painting, like those of the other cells, substance had been lent to an apparition, to an imaginal presence whose light radiated out of the shadows, but only after long concentration, after my attention had shifted away from the window.

Beato Angelico, Noli me tangere, 1440

In particular, the apparition in this first cell was that of the body restored to life after death, the transfigured body *par excellence*, the body of resurrection. And thus an effigy of the goal of all monastic existence, whose task was the patient work of transformation, in that individual man, of the multiple into the One, or the *imitation* of the One—the transformation, the transfiguration of that particular body into its spiritual essence, into the unique and unifying *imago Dei*.

It had not been too difficult to arrive at this point in my reflections. Both conundrums seemed to have been resolved: the reason for the location on that wall and the reason for the presence of that particular image in the first of many cells. But the interpretation had unexpectedly denuded the image, which no longer appeared to me as a representation, but as a presence. My curiosity melted away in the disquiet which that unveiled presence was generating in me. The image was no longer a trace, however sublime, of human history. It was not the memory of a grandeur inherited from the past, a work of art. It was there, immobile, in all its immediate, implacable power. And it spoke to me. It was not an event of the past represented as if on the stage of a theatre where I was a spectator, but an actual event in which I found myself involved.

I left, disoriented. Later on, as I walked through Michelozzo's nearby, silent library, I caught the broken thread of my thoughts. I realized that connecting the painted image with the inhabited space of the cell, with the monk in prayer and in meditation, had cancelled out a distance, a separation in space and time determined by a linguistic convention that conditioned my perception of the image. An unexpected spatial continuum had been created, comprising garden and cell, and I had been included in it. In that unified space, in that very space, must have been generated the event that, evading the convention of representation, reduces the image to an unambiguous signifier, in this case to the simple illustration of a certain episode from the Gospels. My thoughts were all going in the same direction: from the image understood as representation to the image as presence; from the image as story to the image as event in the present, kernel of energy, generator of a transformation: In theological terms: a symbolic, sacramental event, in which time and eternity, known and unknowable, are combined.

Among the illuminated manuscripts of the library, I was reminded of one of Albertus Magnus's theories with which Fra Angelico must have been familiar. Albertus Magnus defined the location as 'active principle of generation', or as '*virtus factiva et operativa*' i.e. power that generates forms, that is expressed in the act of shaping. In other words, the place makes manifest the 'power' of the material, its 'yearning' to take on form (*De Natura Loci*, I,1).

I went back to the cell, to look at the fresco again. Here the location is a garden, an apparently simple garden, but one of which Christ is the gardener: a gardener who tends it carefully, judging by the hoe carried on his shoulder. So there is a close relationship between the garden and its gardener: there would be no gardener without a garden... That place, the garden, is therefore generative; it determines the form in which Christ appears. Moreover, in the nearby *Annunciation*, the portico where Mary is surprised by the angel opens onto an identical garden, evidently the place of transformation in which Christ is destined to carry out his mission—from beginning to end.

Beato Angelico, Annunciation, 1450

Now, after these first thoughts, the red flowers that I saw sprouting in the grass, in the space between the Magdalen and Christ, started to attract my attention, discreetly. Why did Angelico, who would have had no difficulty in painting them in all their detail, depict them, with just a slight movement of the brush, as small red dots, the same kind of round little red dot that he had used for the wounds on Christ's hands and feet. And why are the flowers closest to his feet arranged in groups of five, just as there are five wounds on Christ's body? Or, on the contrary, why did Angelico choose to represent the gardener, at the moment when he was sowing his stigmata in the garden of the world, before returning to his Father? And is it possible that these transfers of significance are secretly controlled by the three small red crosses, painted in that very same shade of red, lined up nearby? Three bloody marks that have no justification in terms of representation, and which seem to allude to the Passion of Christ and perhaps to the Trinity as well.

Fra Angelico's theological master, Thomas Aquinas, said that Christ's wounds are the mark of a special beauty, '*specialis decor*,' the bleeding beauty of humility, which is Beauty itself, the one manifested in the humble lilies of the field and in the Magdalen dressed in red, a lover humbly kneeling in front of her beloved; beauty of the soul that at last contemplates the fountain-head of its love (*Summa theologica* 1938, IIIa,54,4). Perhaps this is why a palm tree is set just above the flowers, forming the axis around which the space of the painting seems to be generated: the palm of eternal life, almost growing amongst the red flowers, sprouting from the bashful, tremulous reaching out and withdrawal of the two hands, the hands of the lover and the beloved. The central tree of five.

What appeared to be an identifiable and definable representation had opened up, from that space filled with flowers in the middle, in a flowering of meaning that let my imagination run free, since it undermined the unambiguous certainty of the significance. Thus I realized with surprise that Angelico had raised the line of the horizon, so that, on close examination, the ground seemed almost to be lifted up and to prevent entry into that space: closed off by a fence at the top, in the distance, but apparently open and welcoming at the front, the place was in fact excluding me.

Perhaps...

I was alone, and timidly tried to assume, in front of the image, the stance of humility suggested by the lover, Mary Magdalene: I kneeled down like her. And looked. The space which had previously seemed closed now opened up: it acquired a coherence of perspective that it had appeared to lack before, and I felt the soul-Magdalen enter it, and move around it, even soaring to the top of the palm.

Now the space of the event was continuous and enfolding: the cell and garden were one and the same, and the soul-Magdalen was introduced into the presence of her transfigured Lord, and thus invited to transfigure herself into his likeness. I was no longer in the same space as before, and I was in another time, both of them articulated by the movements of the imagination. It was not that the image had entered into the time of my existence, as if it were a representation observed and analyzed outside me in the brief space of that spring morning; rather my soul had entered a time and space that were different and unexpected, and yet its own, becoming part of the image, consubstantial with it. Then the image was revealed not as symbol and representation, but as event and presence, an encircling process of assimilation to an essence: now, it had become transformation of the soul in progress.

CHAPTER SEVEN

The Longing for a Mentor

I have been contemplating this subject and wanting to write about it for many years during the course of my work, remembering how often the image of a mentor gets evoked and how, sadly, the absence of one can be missed; how it can be central to the course of any analysis, often announcing itself in the first dream, as in the one below, that contains some images with which to begin.

A young woman, after her first analytical session, dreamed of walking down a tree-covered street. It was a bright day, and the rays of the sun filtered across the greenery. After walking a little way, she came to an open space where a group of youths were standing around painting, some on large paper sheets, some on canvasses, some on a nearby wall. She stood there fascinated, watching them without having the courage to approach them, even though some of them smiled at her and seemed to invite her to sit next to them to see more closely what they were doing. She remembered watching them a long time, as they commented on one or another's paintings. Then she was approached by a man no longer young, who, smiling, had also invited her to look at the paintings. She suddenly told him she didn't know how to paint, and he replied not to worry, that he would teach her.

This man, 'no longer young', who proposed to be her mentor, is one of the reasons that started me thinking about this: the need to differentiate images of the mentor from those of the father, in which the mentor often gets introduced as if he were only a variation of the father, in my judgment with harm to the analysis. Of course there are affinities between mentor and father, but we know also that archetypal forms, as Jung maintained, are not precisely bounded, are not geometric structures. They show themselves in images, immersed in a half-light where the boundaries are unclear, so that the passage from one form to another happens imperceptibly. A similar vision allows us to appreciate the differences by focusing our attention on the more luminous appearances, and at the same time perceive the mixed zones that are emerging from the half-light in which the forms blend. In our case the mixed zone is the expression of authority which both images have in common; authority in the original sense of a conformity to the law, that is, to a form upon which the particular is modelled—a legitimacy that defines the limit, the measure, and confers legitimacy. It determines the difference, as we shall see, the different order to which that authority refers, and the different way in which it comes to be individuated and expressed. Of course the existence of that mixed zone makes it possible for the images to slide together, one on top of the other, in which case the modalities of relationship with the father image might flow into the image of the mentor, sometimes in a contradictory and not always predictable way. Should this occur, the image of the mentor will need to be purified in order to enable it to attract the psyche into its own order of things—which is the 'where', the 'legitimization' that the psyche desires to attain when the longing for the mentor is released in it.

After I wrote this introduction, after I stated succinctly the reasons that led me to reflect on this theme and to consider it worthy of interest even to others, I found myself temporarily unable to continue because of a particular difficulty. This was because I should have stated that the notion of 'mentor' I was proposing seems to have become not only outmoded but almost incomprehensible, as if the luminous emergence of the image, which also represents the possibility for the image to express its own sense, had retreated into shadow. Thus for analysts, the recognition of the mentor seems to have dissolved itself back into the father, whilst the prevailing cultural notion has reduced it to a mere sociological figure, to someone who has the competence to teach, or at best someone who excels in an ability—which is the case in various forms of arts and crafts.

Instead the mentor in question here, even if he can be dressed in these clothes, is not the same as these others: he always goes beyond them, attaining a scope that transcends every social configuration, because his work is not just pedagogical but psychagogical. To understand what I mean, let us recall the aforementioned dream and look at the goal of its longing for a mentor: the question is asked, metaphorically, of the analysis, so that the 'suddenly' begins finally to express itself. I have always had the impression that the nostalgia for a mentor which seizes certain individuals, sometimes throughout their lives, is the result of a regression whose source is not only in personal life but also in today's culture itself. So I found myself in the midst of a more demanding undertaking than the one I first contemplated.To proceed, I must return to an old question, lucidly posited by Jung at the beginning of the 1920s, to which he gave an answer of great, if not complete magnitude; a question that goes against a cultural dominant to which many psychoanalysts were then pledged, who had lost through this a living contact with Jungian thought and practice. I am arguing, and it will shortly be clearer, that a precise distinction between father and mentor is necessary in order to have an adequate rapport with Jungian experience, which otherwise remains inaccessible. Indeed, we should not forget what Jung himself argued regarding the interpretation of archetypal images, that, in the first place, an error in the interpretation damages the interpreter's soul. The question to which I refer regards a hypertrophied valorisation of object relations, to the detriment of an interior life. As we know, Jung did not reduce interior life to mere 'derivatives' of experience, but understood it above all as a conscious relationship with an unknowable depth, or rather with the 'invisibiles' that emerge from it—a discipline that permits a configuration, even if only ephemeral, and the possibility to share it.

In other words an adequate distinction between interior life and valorisation, if not in theory at least in fact, is lost when the image of the mentor is dissolved into that of the father, a figure who presides not in interior life but in relational life— in its hierarchies and the positive knowing that defines them. The mentor is instead someone who introduces us to solitude and to the contemplation of invisibles: a movement that, it is true detaches us from the world, but which is not regressive. There is regression, of course, when detachment follows a state of removal or cutting off from the interior world, such as when the interior world is confined in the Shadow. In this case the invisibles are concretized in archaisms, and then the regression represents the residual form of their influence, the attempt to compensate an interior life missing in reality.

The mentor is not the mediator of the factual world and its laws except indirectly, the opposite of the father. To follow the mentor, the father's point of view should be not just discounted but left behind, as we see when we look at the two images of the mentor that underpin Western culture: Socrates and Jesus. The father's point of view should not be lost, much less remain absent, it is indeed an undeniable presupposition, which, however, will be dethroned through the example of the mentor, whose teaching is constituted in a dialogue with the other point of view. In the testimony of Socrates and Jesus, it becomes evident that attention to the interior world does not bring asocial elitism; quite the contrary. It signifies rather to found the community engagement, that is the care for 'objects', on a law that transcends conventions, opportunities, and personal conveniences, recognizable through a spiritual discipline that installs strong ties with the archetypal virtues that support living together, conceived precisely by these mentors as rooted on lasting foundations. Precisely that connection to these foundations enabled them to be the destroyers of a certain order in the mind, of a system of values that, after Socrates and Jesus, was no longer the same.

Similarly, in the history of an individual, the need for a mentor is felt above all at critical crossroads, when a radical renewal of the personality is necessary, a different orientation of oneself; because the mentor governs exactly the transformation of one state into another, the abandoning of the 'old man' in favour of the 'new man'; from this perspective his appearance in analysis, even at its beginning, in dreams and in the transference, should not surprise us or be misunderstood.

In my work as an analyst, I never intentionally use the process that Jung calls 'amplification'; I follow instead the principle of 'sticking to the image', articulatd by Rafael López-Pedraza and shared by other analysts in archetypal psychology: the images of dreams, fantasies, and memories are irreducible psychic reality, direct manifestations that are at that moment exhaustive of the soul in its indefinable complexities. This is a posture that does not exclude, naturally, recognizing in images the possibility of implying, through their complexity and evocative power, an ulterior disclosing of meaning, to which one responds with attention. An intentional amplification, if we want to call it that, seems to me instead something theoretical, a way for the analyst to expand the actual horizon of comprehension. Instead, by remaining with the image, one may activate the 'return' from the personal to the archetypal, a therapy of the mind already rescued from the fallacy of subjectivism, of personalism, of naturalism, which is predisposed to understand, in analysis, the patient's personal history in the light of their imaginal profundity.

In accordance with this movement I sought in the figure of Socrates as described by Plato some aspects of the image of the mentor and of the disciple in rapport with him. My intention was to achieve a full and informative sketch of this, though I know one runs into the difficulties that are always present when we try to displace ourselves from the existential plane of the encounter—in which is preserved the irreducible otherness, the complexity of the psychic person, the DAIMON—and move to the plane of discourse, which imposes a simplification and a subjective reduction. But the mentors I am discussing have not entrusted the sense of their mission to the written word, relying instead on the persuasive and transforming force of encountering them. Socrates and Jesus, in reality, have no teaching to impart, no established knowledge to transmit; the teaching is their person, their presence. And the metamorphosis, the conversion that is produced in the soul—the realization of their scope—comes about from the way in which we turn to them (Socrates and Jesus), from intimate consonance; we could almost say by empathy, with which we accept their peculiar 'form of existence' and are accepted by it.

These first considerations then begin to clarify a particular of the dream presented above: the mentor invites one to shape oneself, according to that form on which he is himself modelled, thereby seducing with the force of beauty that is shown in this process. The smile of Aphrodite that illumines this dream at every moment and binds the people together, works to assimilate them from many into one. This 'one' in reality is not the mentor, because even the mentor, although before disciples, resembles the Other, which transcends him but which appears through him thanks to that very resemblance. The dream of course does not quite go this far—we find the original understanding of this process in the *Convivio* and *Phaedrus*—but we can retrace in it at least a subtle allusion, an indirect representation of that central and unifying theme of making images, in the surprise that it excites; and in the impulse to imitate that arises from the feeling of incapacity and from the desire to learn; and by virtue of the look that suddenly recognizes its value.

This theme of 'mimesis' constitutes the essence of the encounter between mentor and disciple. We see it most clearly when we return to Socrates, but we can recognize it even if we transport ourselves to the Christian mystical tradition beginning with the texts of John and Paul; not just because these texts depend on a Hellenic culture soaked in Platonism—Platonism, in fact, appears there simply as a disposable cultural instrument, but enough to express even in this new context the movements of the soul that are defined in the mentor/disciple encounter. In fact, mimesis coincides with the *Sequel of God* and the *Assimilation to the Divine (omoiosis to theo* in Greek); and it is around this experience of resemblance, to become like a God—Plato, in the *Phaedrus,* speaks of persuading the lover to become 'like his own God . . . as much as it is possible for a man to have a part of a God' (253 a-b)—it is around this essential articulation of this entire process that the sense of the encounter is played out. 'To resemble his own God' is in fact a metaphor that signifies the process of individuation or the progressive achieving of a form and an implicit measure through an empathic (more aptly called 'erotic') relationship with archetypal images; a process that seems to require the mediation of another human being—the mentor.

If it is true that every soul strives for likeness with a God and is persuaded in this pursuit by love for the mentor, the mentor in his turn becomes a mentor because he shapes himself to a seducing and hence intermediary demon, and therefore an intermediary that awakens in the soul precisely the longing for the God to which it belongs. This demon is Eros, and in the *Symposium* Plato speaks of him in this way:

> As the son of Resource [Poenia] and Need [Poros], it has been his fate to always be needy; nor is he delicate and lovely as most of us believe, but harsh and arid, barefoot and homeless, sleeping on the naked earth, in doorways, or in the very streets beneath the stars of heaven, and always partaking of his mother's poverty. But…he brings his father's resourcefulness to his designs upon the beautiful and the good, for he is gallant, impetuous, and energetic, a mighty hunter, and a master of device and artifice—at once desirous and full of wisdom, a lifelong seeker after truth, an adept in sorcery, enchantment, and seduction. He is neither mortal nor immortal, for in the space of a day he will be now, when all goes well with him, alive and blooming, and now dying, to be born again by virtue of his father's nature, while what he aims will

always ebb away as fast. So Love is never altogether in or out of need, and stands, moreover, midway between ignorance and wisdom (203 d-e).

To this Eros, with the genealogy that explains the characters, Plato was referring the image of Socrates, the mentor. Or perhaps Plato was imagining this mythical form (Eros) through the figure of Socrates as if Eros appeared through him. In any case there is no problem recognizing in this myth—as in the analogous one of the "chariot of the soul" in the *Phaedrus*—the essential nucleus of the Platonic legacy, through which the same thought: and subsequent infinite commentaries seem to be only inexhaustible glosses—beginning with the memorable one of Plotinus, in the fifth chapter of the third *Ennead*. In discussing it, we must remain in a strictly delimited field, keeping in sight the initial scope of these notes.

Socrates, then, is not a 'wise' man but a 'philosopher', or one who desires 'wisdom' precisely because he does not possess it, nor can he possess it. This clear awareness of his poverty is the characteristic from which it is fitting to begin, to reflect on the sense of his presence. He only knows this: that he doesn't know. There is a 'defect' in him that remains because nothing occurs to cure it. And it is to this defect that in the first place he intends to initiate whomever is around him; an absence that is all the more crucial because it does not regard, as a modern person would think, an abstract intellectual knowledge, but rather a concrete knowing, an existential knowing: the correct measure of actions.

In his discourse, in his gentle questioning, Socrates put himself in the role of a man who does not know, a role that his interlocutor initially refutes; so with nice irony he lets the other person display his presumed knowledge—and in so doing he lets the gap between Poverty and Plenty enlarge—and when the interlocutor begins to vacillate, to perceive his inability to reply adequately, Socrates receives him in the same place where he himself lives, the shapeless place of not knowing. It is a state of lostness which follows the shock of losing your presumed knowledge, as if the eye had become inadvertently more acute, had caught the emptiness of that which up till now had seemed a consistent form. Jesus of Nazareth did not move any differently; from his note of penitence he invites repentance, words which share the same root as Penia, Poverty—and to poverty of the spirit, which is really the admission of a failure of light, a darkness of meaning that is the mother of Love.

The process of transformation is announced therefore with a crisis of the preceding certainties, with a hairline fracture of an affirmative identity, thanks to a look that now recognizes the impure infiltration of a shadow that contaminates even the places where values seemed stable: there follows a disorientation, a darkening of the capacity to understand. This *via negativa* is not a choice, and it is not born of conscious intention. It is imposed instead on the will of the ego which resists it, as it resists the presence of the mentor, who at this point is the centre of gravity towards obscurity and indeterminacy, the witness of a failure.

This sometimes almost imperceptible tension, which often accompanies the tales and reflections of patients in analysis—and even the listening and interventions of analysts—and what we mean by the expression 'a resistance' seems to derive, in reality, from the effort of seeking every expedient, of empowering that identity with Poros, Wealth, that the ego tends to assume and keep in order to escape the impending hands of Penia, Poverty—an incessant attempt, heavy with anguish, to find solutions for avoiding the landslide that threatens the compactness of the complex of the 'I'. The risk of certain interpretations—even if they are destined not to be expressed in analysis, which reduce experiences of inadequacy, of defects, of disorientation to concrete present or previous experiences—is to preserve, with expedients of rhetoric, a 'full' feeling of sense rather than by its absence, expanding on an 'empty' one of explanations. The experience of this emptiness is certainly accidental, personal, it can't be represented or recognized except in historical forms in which the individual has lived it; but the causal connection can hide its meaning. Every causal explanation ends up by denying that the failure is the origin rather than the consequence; denying, that is, that the failure is the necessary 'mother'. This is because the same rhetoric of the principle of cause presupposes a 'motor', an artifice, a subject that causes but which could not cause; while the *via negativa* of Socrates discovers that the maternity of the impoverishment does not stop at the beginnings but pervades every breath of a history. In this way the split is dissolved. This discovery happens in fact through the intelligence that penetrates into the unfillable failure of sense, realizing the conjunction that enriches it. So Eros could flash out of it, at the sight of beauty; and beauty will be recognized where otherwise it would remain hidden. This is the knowledge that Socrates grants, erotic knowledge, sudden, and quickly lost. The other kind, stable, is the knowledge of our irreducible 'not knowing'.

The praise of Socrates that Alcibiades articulates at the end of the *Symposium* represents in an exemplary way the events that tie the disciple to the mentor; events destined to remain unfinished in the *Symposium* but also in possible experience, and perhaps in the *Symposium* only because it is thus in possible experience.

Alcibiades says of Socrates that he is very similar to 'one of those little sileni that you see on the statuaries' stalls…modelled with pipes or flutes in their hands, and when you open them down the middle there are little figures of the gods inside' (*Symposium* 215b). He can say this because once he saw the divine images that are inside him, 'so godlike, so golden, so beautiful' (*Symposium* 217a).

It is really this Platonic metaphor, so simple and ordinary, that forms the expression 'interior life' and its meaning. 'Interiors' are the precious likenesses (*agalmata*) of the Gods, hidden in an appearance extraneous to them but visible by virtue of an authentic erotic enthusiasm that is not stopped by the exterior impression but is in search of an interior beauty—and nevertheless, if you look closely, it is not the Gods who are enclosed in Socrates (the soulful look of Eros cannot contemplate the Gods) but as in a mirror their likenesses, their *agalmata,* or the forms of an intermediate, imaginal world, that actually constitutes 'the interior life'.

Recognising in someone the images of the Gods of which one is in search allows us to recognize the mentor and promote the processes of mimesis; but it also allows the mentor to recognize the disciple, in whom those images are equally hidden. An example is in the encounter with Charmides of whom Socrates said, seeing from afar the handsome youth: 'Then, before we see his body, should we not ask him to strip and show us his soul?' (*Charmides* 154e). And speaking of Charmides, having sat down next to him, Socrates says: '…he looked at me in an indescribable manner … and … I caught a sight of the inwards of his garment, and took the flame' (*Charmides* 155c).

Between disciple and mentor then there begins an amorous face-to-face encounter that is a mirror relationship: each seeks in the other what he needs because he is deprived of it, and what he can find only in this 'face-to-face', that is, the image of his own Gods; because it is in conformity with that image, and only with that image, that each of the two recognizes himself to be constituted. Here is the basis of that method that Plato speaks of in the *Alcibiades,* that allows us to 'turn every care to our inferiority' (132b): because 'the soul, if it would know its own self, must turn to another soul' (133b) especially one that resembles its own Gods, and in that one finally look at itself. In the mirror that is the soul of the beloved, there will not appear the face of the lover, but the image of the God that possesses it and constitutes it: his own face and that of the beloved will be illumined by it, as by a flash coming from elsewhere, from another world, beyond the human. Lover and loved one will be joined together, not one to another but each to his place of origin, towards which his nostalgia was heading.

But what happens to the disciple who, like Alcibiades, has seen these images only once? In him there opens up a fault, a split that creates a tension destined not to resolve itself between 'exteriority' and 'interiority', between a world in whose intimacy we are attracted by the beauty that appears from there, but to which we approach, only rarely and briefly, and a world to which we belong, the immediately apparent world in whose indeterminacy it has become impossible to truly recognize oneself. Alcibiades says: 'How moved I felt! In all my soul a sense of irritation and contempt for myself. Oh my slavish life! ... how many times he led me to feel clearly that on my terms life was not worth living! ... how immense were my deficiencies ... The result? With immense force, as if I wanted to flee from the Sirens, I wanted to tape my ears and escape far away... But he produced another effect in me, unique above all. An effect that you would not believe was in me: to have a sense of shame in front of someone. Oh yes! He is the only man who ever made me blush ... And how many times I would have been so happy if I had never cast eyes on this man! To blot him out from the human ledger! And then? I'm absolutely positive my sorrow would have been even greater. In sum with this man here I don't know how to behave' (*Alcibiades* 215e -216f).

The interior life glimpsed in the mentor, its seductive beauty, compels the disciple to revise the basis of his own actions, and he becomes a living problem for himself. His former values and his interest in them are reversed, and he begins to ask himself about how he lived in the past, and how he lives now. There is a point in fact that suddenly becomes clear, through the same way in which everything is begun: it has to do not with an acquirable knowledge but a mode of being which includes the images of the Gods.

To get this Alcibiades desires Socrates, tries to seduce him by the power of his own handsome body, without however succeeding. To change, he wants to include in his own existence the images of the Gods, including Socrates, possessing Socrates. It is really at this moment that the outcome of the encounter between mentor and disciple is decided. Socrates in fact escapes a relationship which would inescapably imprison his own soul in 'exteriority'. He says to Alcibiades: 'You would not be able to find in me some irresistible beauty different from that youthful grace that forms the flower of your own life! Listen: you've seen my beauty and you are trying to have part of it, exchanging with me my beauty for yours... You are trying to acquire, in changing this appearance of yours, a true and proper beauty' (*Alcibiades* 218e).

In this humble way Plato is pointing to the possible destruction that the fascination of the glimpsed images can cause, when, primarily by the mentor, the difference between the interior source of beauty and its exterior mediator is not radically perceived. The experience of the collapse of this difference in analysis (but not only in analysis) confirms the possibility and reality of this destruction. A collapse that produces the shift of the erotic impulse and of 'mimesis' only on the plane of exteriority, that is, on a level that is only personal: from it derive different modes of reciprocal subjugation, in the form of identification, dependence, sexual compulsion. The power of the vision has not disclosed the 'beyond', but exalted *beyond measure* the 'immediate'. And it is really the loss of this measure—or better the lingering in the indeterminacy of exteriority—that is the true result and harm: the hubris, source of evils.

The recollection of his mentor in adolescence by a forty-year-old man at a critical time in his analysis helps me now to take up these same issues, concentrating on a particular experience. And again dreams will introduce the images and decisive emotions, and bring up these memories and reflections, which help us to understand the value that these issues have in a story.

The first two dreams occurred on a night in December. In the first one Signor T was walking through the streets of an unknown city, with the attitude of a tourist who was only vaguely interested, when turning down one street he saw approaching him a small cortege, to which other people were approaching in a festive atmosphere. At the head of the cortege he recognised Pope John, distinguishing him only by his face and expression, because he was dressed as a layman, with a black woolen jacket draped over his shoulders. He was going down the center of the street, followed by people, and he was singing with an expansive voice, one so powerful that it could be distinguished from the chorus that accompanied him. It was a religious chant but triumphant, a chant of victory and enthusiasm. Signor T went toward him crying for joy, happy to be there, and to have so unexpectedly encountered him.

In the second dream of that night, the girlfriend of Signor T came to him one holiday morning. He welcomed her, and only at that moment realized he was shaved, without remembering that he'd done it. He caressed his own cheeks and felt surprised at the smooth skin; he looked in the mirror and saw his face, which had long been hidden by a sizeable and uncut beard, now handsome in a way he never knew before.

Signor T remembered that the day before he had read an article in the newspaper on Pope John—someone he had admired much in his youth—and he was strangely moved at that time by his words encouraging people to restore full dignity to their 'interior life'. In remembering this, Signor T's voice suddenly broke, and then he was silent. He didn't know what to say: we both knew that for fifteen years he had been absorbed in political and professional activity, and that before that day he would have considered the expression 'interior life' to be nothing but the literary residue of other times.

Two days later Signor T dreamed of a youth with whom he identified in the dream, at the same rime remaining an observer. The youth was speaking to his girlfriend of the help that he had given to a rabbi, and of the fact that now he would finally meet and get to know him. He imagined that he would find him benevolent toward himself because of the help that he had given him, and he was all excited by this expectation. The meeting happened in a garden, a sacred and ancient place, like an abandoned cemetery. From the ground rose giant constructions in polished stone, corroded by time, like the pediments of Gothic churches but without decorations. All this the youth, and with him Signor T, could only remember afterwards, because at the moment of his meeting he was so seized by emotion, he had hardly noticed that unknown place. It was twilight. There was an atmosphere of containment about it, silent. He felt, without seeing it, the presence of a wall all around it. The rabbi came out from behind one of the pediments and spoke only briefly with the youth. Very carefully he wrote on a piece of paper two numbers corresponding to the payment he expected from the youth. He totaled the sum, paid the bill, and with a brief salute he went off. The youth was disappointed: he would have wished for more personal consideration, some recognition; he knew well the courage it took for him to be on the side of a Jew. His girlfriend smiled at him and that smile consoled him a little. He began then to roam around the garden; he looked at the great pediments lined up one behind the other, perhaps three of them, perhaps more, and then the smaller ones. Suddenly he was seized by awe for those solemn presences which appeared to him like ancient prayers in stone. And at the end he understood—moved so much that he woke up—that this had been the real payment: to come to the garden of which the rabbi was the custodian.

Signor T felt that this dream represented an aspect hitherto not considered by his analysis. The great pediments excited in him a 'sacred fear', as he said, for their unexpected nearness, for their mysterious emergence from ground and shadow. Permanence in this garden would have been unsustainable beyond the brief time that was allotted to him there. Yet it would never be forgotten. Thinking of his analysis he considered how difficult it had been for him to affirm the value of analysis in the cultural milieu in which he lived, whose values and prejudices he shared. He had understood at least a little, he said smiling, how one can feel being a Jew among Gentiles. He turned over in his mind the deep emotion he had felt some days before at the thought of 'the interior life', and it seemed to him that the garden could in some way be representative of it. And perhaps for a while it seemed to him that his analyst was like a rabbi in a country of Catholics... but no longer now. Now it seemed to him that the rabbi, who was the guardian of that sacred place, was like the pediments, he lived there independently of the analyst and the analysis. The analysis had been the way to find that place. At first the place of the analysis must have made a similar impression on him, for arriving there had been like entering into an unsettling mystery. Now everything was more familiar but that place had not disappeared yet: perhaps he had found his true place.

The next day, which was also the day following the session in which we had discussed this dream, Signor T had another dream: he was walking up and down a street from his youth, when he recognized, among the other boys, Arturo, a friend from those far-off days. He had the beardless face of back then, handsome, and also as then he had a look that radiated with intelligence.

Signor T had not thought about Arturo in many years and was surprised to find him now in a dream, he knew that he had abandoned a university career which was barely begun, to pursue his ideal life among 'the damned of the earth'—'as he used to say', he added with irony. But fifteen days had to pass before the connections that had evoked this personage, still unforeseeably alive in his soul, could be understood by Signor T. On the night of one of the last days of December, Signor T dreamed of turning down an alley and running into Arturo again. He remembered having met him in his dream of several nights ago, and now he found him really looking like he had already dreamt: he studied his smiling face for a moment and noticed clearly the lines, while the background almost dissolved, so as to give greater prominence to the face which he intensely scrutinized and recognized.

This precise focusing of the image and his sense of 'ulterior' reality in regard to that of the dream let fall a veil, and now the first two dreams that I have discussed here became more understandable. His own face without his beard in the second dream, in fact, appeared now to Signor T very similar to Arturo's in that dream; and the black woolen coat on the shoulders of Pope John reminded him of a teacher that he and Arturo and other boys like them used to see at his school. He began then to speak with great emotion of this man, who in those days had been his point of reference for the term 'interior life'—a mentor of 'interior life'. Those were years full of enthusiasm, of ideals created by that association with the teacher; and Arturo, a little older than Signor T, was his most sought-after friend; cultivated, courageous, noble-hearted. In the parochial atmosphere where he lived, however, the teacher was viewed with hostility, marginalized, sometimes even slandered, and people tried to warn the boys away from his 'dangerous' influence. But the teacher told them to walk with their heads high, to take for their role models only the great men and to fear nothing but their own consciences. Nonetheless Signor T, though he loved this man, had begun to distance himself from him, had begun to lose his enthusiasm, until it was finally just extinguished. The need to be like all the others had prevailed in him to the point of sharing certain judgments of the denigrators of the teacher. The voice of Signor T became pitiless, full of sorrow and shame. Commenting on the first dream he said: 'After that time it seems I never sang any more, only argued and chattered'. It was a sorrow that carried away, as in the dream, the uncut beard with which he hid his true face, the beauty which maybe now he could begin to see.

I saw him again several days later, during the first week in January. He had dreamed of being seated in a restaurant under a pergola together with Professor C. It was dim, at twilight. Professor C spoke with enthusiasm of a recent archaeological discovery and showed him a detailed sketch made precisely to illustrate to Signor T what had been discovered. At first the sketch seemed incomprehensible, but then Signor T began to adjust to it, while the sketch itself was undergoing a metamorphosis, changing from the initial abstract scheme into a photograph, and then directly into the real thing: a poor little hut that was very old. This progressive and unexpected immersion into the image brought joy to Signor T, feeling that he had himself discovered what was interesting to see and know there. The hut had a primitive aspect, constructed with rough stones, and on one side it had a tombstone on which was inscribed, quite visible in the daylight, a Greek cross carved in stone. Professor C said, fascinated by the vision, that this was surely the origin of the cross that bakers always carve on the top of bread. Signor T, instead, said that this, like the cross on bread, was a memory of the cross marked on the doors of the Hebrews on the night before their exodus from Egypt. It was the cross that distinguished the Hebrew houses from other people's, preserving them from the vengeance of God. It was therefore a mark of discrimination and recognition, one that was repeated on this house in stone and with the same significance. In saying all this Signor T smiled at Professor C and felt at peace.

Signor T hung around with Professor C for a few months, suddenly appreciating his intelligence and culture, though for some time it had left him perplexed. It seemed to him that in the end every thought he had, all his knowledge, went above all to build his prestige. With a certain discomfort Signor T recognized now in this person and in the ambiguous fascination that emanated from him, the secret essence of what he himself had been seeking, perhaps up until the time he had abandoned his mentor—paraphrasing Plato, 'he had sought to seem, not to be, just.' The conflict of interpretations in the second part of the dream suggested exactly this difference. The interpretation given by Signor T signaled his interior surrender, welcoming the necessity of the exodus, of following his own God, which once he had seen in the mentor. And now the re-evocation of the mentor made the choice easier, the passage from 'old man' to 'new man'.

Two weeks later the old mentor appeared at last in a dream. And then he came back many times, for a year, as if to accompany a return not to him but to that dark light that through him had illuminated the adolescent Signor T.

After an automobile trip, Signor T and his girlfriend in the dream had arrived at night at an isolated house. Inside the house, seated at a table, with his head held in his hands in a melancholy attitude, was the mentor of his youth. He seemed the same as twenty-five years before, and suddenly he recognized Signor T. The two smiled, and Signor T felt an impulse of profound affection for him and said to him movingly that he had been really important for his life. The face of the mentor lit up, as if he had been waiting a long time for that recognition, and smiled happily. Signor T went away. When he returned, he found the mentor sinking into a circular opening in the pavement, immersed up to his neck in a dirty liquid that filled the hole. He smiled sweetly, a humble look. Signor T was moved, because he knew that with that gesture the mentor wanted to mortify his own pride which had been excited by his recognition. Afterwards Signor T climbed a winding staircase with his girlfriend and with her sang a religious hymn in a loud voice. Slowly as the song proceeded, Signor T began to realise with immense joy that he was capable of singing. The emotion made him sob, but the song went on nonetheless with surging force, and his whole body swayed with the music.

The song that in the first dream had drawn Signor T—and that sprang from a far-off mentor—now surrounded him, like an unexpected gift; a song of devotion to his God, while his mentor went back into nothingness. A passage of Kierkegaard comes to mind: 'The disciple is the opportunity for the mentor to understand himself, and vice versa the mentor is the opportunity for the disciple to understand himself. At the mentor's death he does not leave behind any trace of himself in the soul of the disciple, precisely as (and so much less) the disciple cannot pretend that the mentor is indebted to him for something... because only he understands Socrates best who understands that he owes nothing to Socrates, something that Socrates himself prefers and that is beautiful to have been able to want' (Kierkegaard 1972, p. 232).

Up till now I have been speaking of 'mentor' and 'disciple' because these are the usual terms; understandably because this is how the terms are conceived by the disciple, by his longing, by his gratitude, by his nostalgia. But these are not the terms of the mentor; Socrates and Jesus prefer the word 'friends', and the essential form of the encounter with them is, as we have seen, resemblance. Moreover, if the emotion that animates the student is not brought on by the friendship of the mentor, if it is not itself transformed into friendship, it ends with the deepening of a split—on one side obscurity, the night of the meaning, on the other the light of wisdom. Perhaps here is where gets born the fantasy of an 'old sage' who knows the immanent meaning of reality, who holds power over things because he knows the meaning hidden there, and guides the budding personality towards its completion. A supposition, this, that would open up a new chapter, because it would demand a long and appropriate meditation on all that Jung has said on this subject. Instead I will now bring this reflection to a close.

It is fitting to conclude this essay by turning to the meaning for the psyche of the relationship between mentor and disciple, and to ask what irreducible necessity of the soul this relation is coping with. And here, too, a dream can be of help, the dream that a man of forty-six had at the end of a long analysis. After waking—in the dream—he was leaving his house to begin the new day. He stopped next to the door to look in the mirror; or better, he saw himself going through this routine act as if a second ego was on the shoulders of the one who was doing it. The ego that did it did not see in the mirror anything but the usual image of his face, while the ego behind his shoulders, in place of the usual face, saw a resplendent face with a beauty never seen before, like the face of an angel. The emotion for this unexpected, unsustainable vision was so intense that the man woke up frightened.

The encounter between mentor and disciple has perhaps for its final purpose the constituting or reconstituting of this dyad that the dream reveals: on one side the imaginal ego—that aspect of the ego complex that mediates in the ego the relationship with the imaginal world—on the other side the face of the angel, the image of the God to whom the soul belongs. As the dream shows, this dyad is not in its essence stable; because the divine, the beyond-the-human, is ungraspable, it eludes history. Or it manifests itself in time, in a fleeting moment, in the fluttering wings of an annunciation. This is the teaching of the mentor that keeps the student at the ridge which divides light and shadow, time and eternity, and defines its doubleness, through which, like Socrates, 'he is and he is not', and thus becomes realized as a symbolic individual. I think Jung had this in mind when he proposed the metaphor of the Self as a center of gravity that holds together (and separate) consciousness and unconsciousness, and whose loss, with relative collapse of the difference, condemns the ego to unbalance and excess, to inflation as well as to deflation.

A mentor is necessary for us, one who recognizes in us the fleeting appearance of the angel, a mentor whose own vision helps us to see in his likeness—in the likeness of Eros. It is enough sometimes to notice the unspeakable beauty of the Face to find the lost sense of a dignity and a simply human measure, to be who we are, in our house, on our street. There is needed no more than a flash—however little we can endure everything else—for illuminating and recognizing the horizon that contains us. Individuation begins with that flash—whatever be the moment in which it happens and at times it happens even in infancy—and it continues like a road in the dark, which other flashes, sometimes only briefly, illuminate. These illuminations of beauty draw us into transformations that in the splendor of a form find their beginning and draw us to the 'beyond' towards which Eros is pointing.

CHAPTER EIGHT

Unity in Multiplicity

Several years ago, an elderly British analyst who had come to Florence for a seminar on the Self told us that during his training he had been urged not to risk talking about the Self before he had attained the wisdom of old age. In fact the Self was considered beyond the grasp of a young man, and even of one who was not really old. And he added that at that time people spoke about the process of individuation as if it were a course at the polytechnic, with phases and passages of growing complexity that would not reach their conclusion until old age. His comments were cheerful, ironic, and yet, while he based his reasoning about the Self on a subtle and erudite reference to the theology of Meister Eckhart, it occurred to me that those teachings were not so unfounded, if even he felt it necessary to resort to such unfathomable visions, to the impenetrable relationship between the Persons of the Trinity, or rather to the way it had been conceived by that great mediaeval mystic. Once again, the Self was being represented in a majestic form, in the likeness of the biblical God, a creator God. As Jung had done, going so far as not only to define the Self as 'an *a priori* existent out of which the ego evolves' (Jung 1955b, par. 391), but also to claim that its symbols, the symbols of unity and totality, 'can no longer be distinguished from the *imago*

Dei', and that 'all statements about the God-image apply also to the empirical symbols of totality' (Jung 1959, par. 31).

But is the creative totality described by Trinitarian theology, integrated with Jung's speculations on the Fourth Person, really the archetypal mirror in which a human being is expected to recognize the presence and action of the Self? Can that dark impulse towards form (Jung 1954b,2, par. 402) which generates and sustains the process of individuation really be embodied in the will of the biblical God, in his plan for humanity?

I recall one of my first patients: he was my own age, around thirty, and a musician who taught at secondary school. He led a very quiet life, shy of any contact, and was afraid of his pupils, whom he faced every day as if they were a hydra with thirty heads: that was how he put it. We were still at the beginning of the analysis when one day he came into the consulting room, looked around with obvious astonishment, sat down in front of me and burst out: 'But what have you done? Have you sawn off the legs of the furniture?' I stared at him, bewildered in my turn at his question. He went on: 'Everything is lower than the other times... the table, the bookcase, the chairs... everything lower...' The discussion of that surprising event brought to the surface the crushing feeling of weakness and humiliation that had hitherto shaped his existence. He then told me about a dream he had just had. He was in a room, in the middle of a crowd that was moving around in a confused manner: he felt suffocated and overwhelmed. Suddenly, he realized that Pope John was passing by, smiling. He thought: 'If only I could touch him!' The pope had turned in his direction, as if he had heard him, and extended an arm towards him. He too had stretched out one arm, to reach the pope's through the throng. And so the tip of the pope's index finger had been able to touch the tip of the index finger that he had extended, and a powerful flow of energy had passed between them at the moment of contact, filling him with new life. Then the pope had moved away and he had woken up with an unaccustomed feeling of strength, well-being and trust. That contact had reminded him, he told me, of the contact between God the Creator and Adam on the ceiling of the Sistine Chapel.

The dream explained what had happened at the beginning of the session: as a result of that influx of energy, the man had regained his true height, and no longer needed to feel he was a worthless presence, at least in the analyst's consulting room. It seemed that the gesture in the dream had created a symbol: the reunion of the creature with the creator in the reunion of the lost son with the Holy

Father—the man had once been a staunch Catholic. Whence its power.

Reconsidering this image today, we can find many clues as to the state the man found himself in, commencing with the vague presences that were suffocating him and blocking his contact with the pope. We could even see it as an expression of the hopes he had placed in the analytical relationship, or as a defence against the exposure of his weakness in analysis. But while not excluding the complex resonances implied by this dream, like any other, we can set store above all by the hypothesis that it prefigured the reunion of the ego with the generative and regenerative power of the Self; and thus the healing of a chronic sense of exile and isolation, through a symbolic representation that, even in its details, appears to justify the theological speculations of Jung and many of his followers.

I was not sympathetic towards those speculations, however, and was to become even less so later on. Above all I was suspicious of any image of completeness and wholeness, of any ideal goal. Perhaps because I was not a wise old man (and even after many years still am not), or perhaps because existentialist thought, to which I had been attracted since my adolescence, had taken me in other directions, and had placed the values to which I looked elsewhere.

Support for me, in my frame of mind at that time and in my reflections, came from a short text, *Failure and Analysis*, which James Hillman had written not long before. I remember reading it over and over again, especially the concluding page:

> We may do more justice with the failures in analysis and the failure of analysis, when we consider analysis as a process in failure and even individuation as a movement in the realm of Hades, invisibly, where the literalisms of life are reflected in the metaphors of death. Then individuation, the uniqueness of individual personalities, will be recognized as Unamuno characterized it in the tragic sense of life, which has its own joy, its own comedy.
>
> When I am in despair, I do not want to be told of re-birth; when I am aging and decaying and the civilization around me collapsing from its over-growth that is over-kill, I cannot tolerate that word "growth", and when I am falling to bits in my complexities, I cannot abide the defensive simplistics of mandalas, nor the sentimentalities of individuation as unity and wholeness. These are formulae presented through a fantasy of opposites—the disintegration shall be compensated

> by integration. But what of cure through likeness, where like takes care of like? I want the right background to the failure of life; I want to hear with precision of those Gods who are served by and thrive upon and can hence provide an archetypal background and even an eros connection with the defeat, decay and dismemberment, because these dominants would reflect the *experienced* psyche (not in its Aristotelian conceptualization as belonging to life), but in the actuality of its only known goal which is also both its way and its substance: death (Hillman 1972, p.6).

I read and re-read that essay, and this passage in particular, since it responded in a surprising way to an anxiety of mine, to which I had tried to give expression in several articles with a marked emphasis on death, weakness and transience. Thoughts so insistent, I reflected, and echoing from places very far apart, might stem from a single unconscious fantasy, destined to wear down established defensive structures. Those structures, moreover, could be considered not just fortuitous, but also the expression of a cultural orientation that to the anguish of fragmentation and transience opposes a cohesion, attained through a persona wholly dependent on social recognition; and so, never truly adequate and thus exposed to the anxiety of failure and to repeated, inevitable collapses. This ideal goal, of cohesion and coherence, in fact produced the exaltation of a subject who was its architect, the maximum enhancement of the superiority of the egoic consciousness and project, and of a will, of a discipline capable of imposing the necessary order, following deep-rooted cultural models; and it seemed to me that this same goal was shared by the practice of analysis, at least as I had understood it up to that point, but that was also proving fallacious and doomed to painful collapse.

However, it should be said that Jung too, in a passage in *Aion*, had already come to regard certain symbols of order as an expression of a defensive structure in embryo: 'Experience shows that individual mandalas are symbols of *order*, and that they occur in patients principally during times of psychic disorientation or re-orientation. As magic circles they bind and subdue the lawless powers belonging to the world of darkness, and depict or create an order that transforms the chaos into a cosmos' (Jung 1959, par. 60). What Jung was referring to was, on close examination, the traumatic formation of a complex: from the overwhelming and unnameable powers that are its origin to the archetypal response with which the soul attempts to limit its destructive effects, by including them in a system of meaning that transforms the alien and intolerable into experience. A defensive process like this is bound to involve a part of the psyche that will remain assimilated to the emerging archaic form, deriving an undifferentiated power from it; to some extent suited to defence, but at the expense of other and more everyday needs, for which not enough energy will be left. This complex state makes it unlikely that that archaic form will come to be elaborated to the point where its meaning is reached, so that it becomes a differentiated and integrated mode of experience. Although this possibility should not be completely dismissed: Jung makes this clear in the continuation of that passage: 'The mandala at first comes into the conscious mind as an unimpressive point or dot, and a great deal of hard and painstaking work as well as the integration of many projections are generally required before the full range of the symbol can be anything like completely understood' (Jung 1959, par. 60).

This means, in fact, that its initial manifestation is archaic, and independent of both the ego and the whole of the psyche, into which it can only be integrated after adequate assimilation and elaboration. This integration, however, will not take place because one has succeeded in conceiving or recognizing a form that symbolizes an all-inclusive order, a totality, a calming harmony of the whole, and not even because one has set up an ideal for which to aim; but when, as I prefer to think, the possibility of the form has gradually matured, in other words the capacity to bring to completion, in their complexity, those possibilities of the individual existence that were previously only barely revealed, by hints and in fragments. It seems to me that only in the course of such a process is the autonomy of the complex dissolved, and that the archetypal defences, as will become clearer later on, are diluted in an action that is of use to the psyche as a whole: fashioning the order in which the possible can sometimes flourish and find its form.

Usually, however, elaboration and assimilation remain included in the defensive function, subordinate to it in part for the dissociated character of the images involved: 'If this understanding', Jung wrote in fact, 'were purely intellectual it would be achieved without much difficulty ….' But psychological experience 'demonstrates as plainly as could be wished that the intellectual "grasp" of a psychological fact produces no more than a concept of it, and that a concept is no more than a name, a *flatus vocis*' (Jung 1959, par. 60). In other words, a conceptual reduction of the reality of the soul, which in the schizoid state in particular, is wrongly celebrated as an achievement. This question is decisive, since it regards the very possibility of elaborating and assimilating an archetypal response, and thus dissolving the autonomy of a complex; a possibility that for Jung is linked to an adequate functioning of the feelings, or perhaps it would be better to say to a capacity for empathy. Nevertheless, the latter manages to be truly effective if new factors intervene to catalyze a transformation of what has remained static and unilateral precisely in so far as it is a defensive structure—a question that we will be able to examine better further on.

In 1971 Hillman published another essay, *Psychology: Monotheistic or Polytheistic?*, in which he put forward a critique of the theological conception of the Self—the Self understood as final stage and goal of the process of individuation (Hillman 1971). I was not yet capable of understanding the subtle and complex implications of that essay, which was to prove a milestone in critical reflection within the field of Jungian psychology. But it certainly left me with thoughts that influenced the directions I went in subsequently, so that I can read it again now with particular appreciation.

Hillman asked himself what kind of consciousness it was that perceived psychic life in terms of stages, of development and of goal; in other words, what specific archetypal model finds expression in the Jungian conception and descriptions of the Self. And he concluded that the Self, as it is usually presented, seems rather to be an expression of the Wise Old Man. *Senex* consciousness, in fact, is manifested essentially in those images of order that are usually ascribed to the Self, and thus in geometric figures, crystals and stones, and in abstractions that tend to dissolve the images; while the behaviour that corresponds to this consciousness, and the process that leads to it, are reflected in metaphors of introversion, and thus in a tendency to detachment from the sensible world. In Hillman's view again, we owe to this consciousness both the customary conception of the Self and the monotheistic vision, with their assurance of including and resolving the contradictions that the multiplicity of complexes and the polytheistic pandemonium would instead maintain free and unopposed; and thus of bringing about an order that will put an end to chaos. This consciousness could also be represented as a piece of land that has emerged entirely from the sea of the unconscious, from which it has excluded and isolated itself and which it now views from a distance and from above.

The consciousness of syzygy—the coupling of animus and anima, which in Jung's later writings, and *Aion* in particular, is placed at the origin of the polytheistic imagination, i.e. of imagination *tout court*—on the contrary appears inclusive, like an archipelago in which land and sea, while distinct, are contiguous and permeable. It is due to the preservation of this intimate and undefined relationship between 'consciousness' and 'unconscious' that the languages of the soul and psychology are metaphorical, to the point of transforming even those conceptual formulations whose meaning seems unambiguous into metaphors. In fact, while the *senex* sees thing in a monocular perspective, and thus organizes the various phenomena into a unitary space with a single point of view, syzygy is characterized by a multiplicity of coexisting points of view, which cannot be equated with one another but are all related, and so semantic ambiguity is typical of it. Syzygy, in fact, reflects a polycentric psyche, which manifests itself in a multiplicity of partial consciousnesses, similar to stars or sparks (Jung 1954b,2, pars. 388-396), not necessarily destined to fuse into a higher consciousness, in whose light the partial luminosities are dissolved. That more intense luminosity can only be generated in a process that by correcting and normalizing, integrating and expanding, arranges experiences into a hierarchy, and particulars into a harmonious whole. While the vague and intermittent consciousness of syzygy permits the establishment of an order that is not conclusive, like that of the *senex*, but open; an order which is realized in the opening up to the possible, and thus does not reassure but is fraught with uncertainty and hope.

In a psyche conceived as polycentric, Hillman argued in that essay, '...each complex deserves its respect in its own right. In this circularity, there seem no preferred positions, no sure statements about positive and negative, and therefore no need to rule out some configurations and *topoi* as "pathological"' (Hillman 1971, p. 198). In fact, when *senex* consciousness, responsible for the original conception of individuation and analysis, gives way to the consciousness proper to syzygy, i.e. to a polytheistic vision of psychic life, the fundamental idea of progress by hierarchical stages, again according to Hillman, is spontaneously put aside, and the consequence of this is 'more tolerance for the non-growth, non-upward, and non-ordered components of the psyche' as '[t]here is more room for variance when there is more place given to variety'. And in particular, where the question of a theological or psychological conception of the Self is concerned, it becomes clear that 'many of the judgments which have previously been called psychological were rather theological'; in other words they were 'statements about dreams and fantasies and behaviour, and people too, coming from a monotheistic ideal of wholeness (the Self)' that devalues the primal multiplicity of souls, 'a theological wholeness, where individuation manifests according to degrees of approximation to an ideal of unity' (Hillman, 1971, p. 199).

From the perspective of syzygy, therefore, the Self of which we are speaking does not appear as the totality of the psyche, i.e. as the completion of the process by which it would be individuated; rather it seems to be a special complex, whose emotions and fantasies tend to bring the multiplicity of the psyche within the perspective of a unified consciousness, in order to constitute an orderly design of the world that would provide a certainty of orientation, and to determine a consistent and unambiguous pattern of behaviour where even opposites, when they emerge, are able to coexist in an orderly way. Precisely because of these characteristics, however, it appears as a complex that tends dangerously towards unilaterality, which attempts to lay down laws and de-legitimize fantasies, emotions and patterns of behaviour not in keeping with the order that is being established in the psyche. Thus it can exert a repressive violence that causes inner traumas, capable of triggering the splitting of other complexes from the whole.

Not that it necessarily leads to these results: it does so to the extent to which it becomes hypertrophied, with an overpowering charge of energy, something which fosters the tendency to place oneself on the top of the mountain, in a position of pre-eminence, of superiority; if, that is, it is transformed into an autonomous and prescriptive personality, one that tends, in a totalitarian manner, to assimilate or subjugate the other partial personalities, obliterating them or at any rate playing down their point of view; or, to put it another way, if it tends to focus psychic energy, not to squander it in inner conflicts, prematurely realizing a unity at the expense of whatever appears discordant, which is amputated. All this happens, as we have seen, when it is structured to meet a defensive need. The partial personality that dominates the scene in this case, dissociated and autonomous, manifests itself with the archetypal characteristics of the 'Personality', of the Great Man: Wise Old Man, Sacred Monarch, Master; thus it is an embodiment of autonomy itself, of the Author, or at least the custodian of the Law, supreme judge and sole authorized interpreter. And naturally this personality can be projected, for example, onto a charismatic leader, or the ego may be assimilated and identified with it.

At this point in my reflections, I think it is at last possible to understand an otherwise obscure statement, made on one of the last pages of *Aion*: 'The recognition of anima and animus is a specific experience that seems to be reserved mostly, or at any rate primarily, for psychotherapists (Jung 1959, par. 424). In other words, syzygy is the form of consciousness proper to a psychotherapist; it would in fact be the point of view that focuses the attention and interest not on the whole and the constant, but on the particular, on the temporary which is different each time, and thus renders them capable of penetrating into individual emotions, into individual images, in the complexity of relations, and of carefully reflecting the illusions, tangles and ambiguities of the soul.

Syzygy deconstructs the uniform and multiplies the points of view, adhering to a complexity of the real that it does not simplify or curtail, but underlines and exalts. In the first place it recognizes a field where different, independent and irreducible powers come to the surface, and its movement from one to the other is a circumambulation, which means distinguishing and recognizing a predominant value in difference, in particularity, in establishing multiple and complicated relationships, and not in assimilating and unifying, in congealing, in making things the same, as the *senex* consciousness does. The latter seems typical instead of a philosopher, theologian or naturalist, since it produces an inclination to subordinate the dispersion of the sensible, through reflection, to an orderly and unitary vision; in other words, it incites a discipline of the spirit aimed at fitting the experience of the psyche into the categories or the style of the natural sciences, philosophy or theology, as sometimes happens with the speculation of analytical psychology as well.

The intensified awareness of the particular, however, does not exclude the constitution of a unitary sense and a meaning that has a general value; however, it is a 'truth' that is revealed by the particular itself, in the ungraspable moment of its resplendence, and then is left to its transcendent fate. So through the particular it becomes possible to experience a stable foundation 'piece by piece', on the strength of an archetypal memory that cannot be made available in concepts without being lost, but can be represented in images that symbolize its action and are a further manifestation of it. This process induces an understanding in narrative form, 'a dramatic, mythological way of thinking and speaking' (Jung 1959, par. 25), which for Jung is the best suited to the living psyche, since 'every psychic process, so far as it can be observed as such, is essentially *theoria*, that is to say, it is a *presentation*; and its reconstruction—or "re-presentation"—is at best only *a variant of the same presentation*' (Jung 1954, par. 162).

The year after the publication of *Aion*, Jung commented on the style of his writing in a letter he wrote to Werblowsky on 17 June 1952:

> The language I speak must be ambiguous, must have two meanings, in order to do justice to the dual aspect of our psychic nature. I strive quite consciously and deliberately for ambiguity of expression, because it is superior to unequivocalness and reflects the nature of life .... I purposely allow all the overtones and undertones to be heard, partly because they are there anyway, and partly because they give a fuller picture of reality .... That is why I prefer ambiguous language, since it does equal justice to the subjectivity of the archetypal idea and to the autonomy of the archetype.... The realm of the psyche is immeasurably great and filled with living reality [and] it is the frame within which I can express my experience' (Jung 1976a, pp. 70-71).

What makes possible, if such a thing is possible, the dissolving of the emotions and fantasies encysted in an autonomous complex, and their fluidization in mental life? What is it that favours, in analysis, the weakening of a complex as defensive construct, and makes possible the flow of its energy, hitherto confined in a personification with archaic characteristics? In particular when it stands, as we have seen with the complex of the Self, as a dominator, a split nucleus of omnipotence, that leaves the rest of the psyche in a state of weakness, dependence and disorientation, and in consequent need of a stable centre, inside or outside, which can constantly be referred to.

The case history that I began to record earlier may be of some assistance in the attempt to answer these questions.

From the beginning, I recall chiefly stories of solitude, of isolation within the family and the village. A poor village in the country, a peasant family without any education; and he, who as a child used to wear his grandfather's wide-brimmed hat at a rakish angle, so as to mimic in the mirror a photograph of Giacomo Puccini, the musical idol of his part of the world. He dreamed about making music, but it had all been confined to his fantasies until the parish priest became aware of his passion, and had begun to teach him to play the harmonium. The priest had persuaded his father to let him carry on his studies at the conservatory in a nearby town, where attendance meant that he had to stay until evening. An adolescence devoted exclusively to his dream, while he watched from a distance his fellow teenagers, frivolous, irresponsible and greedy for pleasure. His only pleasure, music. Destined to be as well as to feel himself different, extraneous to the company of other adolescents, who got together to play football or to dance, while he shut himself up for hours in church, where by now he could play the organ too. Unable to relate to his fellows in the town, unable to relate to his fellows in the village. He looked at girls with desire, but from a distance; they seemed unattainable and aggressive, and to approach them he would have had to be like those bold and playful young men who were able to make them laugh. Both sexes may even have thought he was homosexual, timid as he was, always playing the organ in church when he came back from the city in the evening. Prey to this suspicion, he passed hours in indescribable anguish. In his village men didn't go to church and from adolescence frequented the 'club', where they played cards and learned to smoke and swear. As for music, all they knew and sang were popular songs, or preferably the dirty ditties of the tavern; while he went to church and played church music.

After a few years, he moved from the provincial conservatory to one in a bigger city, another long journey to be made every day. The teachers there seemed more cultivated, often playing abroad, and instilled in their students the need for a purified and abstract music: away with narration, away with sentiment, away with melodic lines, their place taken by atonal, rarefied languages, by complex, difficult serial constructions that made no concessions to the pleasure of listening... He had started to follow one of these teachers, had sought to absorb all his ideas, not just about music but about anthroposophy too, and had studied, on his suggestion, the books of Rudolf Steiner translated into Italian. Music was a higher manifestation of the spirit, it was the echo of a forgotten cosmic harmony, and a musician would be better able to compose it the more his spirit had been elevated, the more he had been initiated into the mysteries of wisdom. The teacher, or rather the maestro, as he called him, was surrounded by pupils who hung on his every word. Only rarely did he compose music, but those few pages were sublime... Or at least that was what his disciples murmured.

The young musician had begun to compose with ever increasing difficulty: a few minutes of music was an almost unattainable goal, and the music was never pure enough; only for brief moments did it draw on the higher spheres of the spirit. With a desperate effort, and ashamed at a mediocrity that seemed obvious to his eyes, albeit benevolently tolerated by the maestro, he had managed to pass the final examinations of his course of study. Leaving the conservatory, he had continued to frequent the maestro, from whom he awaited the teachings that would at last give him access to true music. But he had stopped composing. He entered the classes where he had started to teach with terror. He desired a woman, but no longer dared approach her, after several humiliating failures. Finally he had come to me, after a visit to a psychiatric clinic which had been forced on him by an unbearable state of anxiety.

This account of mine interprets the memory of inner events related by my patient over the course of our first sessions, in bitter words that often expressed feelings of anger and contempt towards their protagonist, who appeared very different from the young man I was observing at that moment: soberly dressed, tall, lean, proud in demeanour but with no sign of ostentation, detached if not downright suspicious, but whose expression revealed, every now and then, flashes of tenderness.

When we came to comment on the dream, our musician started to speak to me with growing disparagement of Pope John, who at that time was still very much alive in the popular imagination. As he gradually distanced himself from the impression created by the dream and immersed himself in more familiar thoughts as he talked, he came up with more and more remarks belittling his value, until the figure of the previous pope, Pius XII, emerged in comparison. It was immediately apparent that his hieratic figure held a grip on his imagination: distant from everyone, unreachable by the crowd who watched him from afar, and who kneeled on his appearance to obtain his solemn blessing. His voice came down to the faithful from on high, his words were firm and final. Austere and brusque in manner; spiritual man *par excellence*; strict and inflexible judge; feared and exalted. But above all, infallible guide. His figure, emerging in this way, had overshadowed that of Pope John, a good, plump and simple man who might have been one of the old men of his village. Those modest speeches of his, reflecting no more than an elementary culture; and those people thronged around him, as in the dream, with their unbearable familiarity, as if he were a good-natured grandpa: everything, in his presence, was prosaic, banal, ordinary. When all is said and done: a sentimentalist without spiritual stature. A similar assessment to the one he now made of Puccini, so deeply loved in his adolescence and yet almost forgotten.

I believe that that first time everything slipped by without further comment, from him or me. Only later did it become clear, and even clearer now that I am writing about it many years afterwards, that it marked the beginning of a process destined to depose the old monarch and replace him with the new one, inspired not by a desire for distance and superior self-sufficiency, but for sensitive and warm relationship. A process that would take the monarch out of his isolation, and bring him closer to the many, into which he then appeared to dissolve. The energy that had flowed from the pope to the young man through that fleeting contact in the dream had begun to be redeployed, to diffuse into the soul, to give a keen sense of importance even to those aspects that he had done without for too long.

How different from this dream, and from the events that ensued, was the dream that another patient related to me in those days. He too was in a place frequented by many people, a place of transit and movement, a railway station. But he was too frightened at the thought of any close contact, even the casual ones of a public place, and he also feared the irruption of unknown forces: so he had traced a circle around himself with a stick, in order to keep everything and everyone at a distance. It was the last dream he recounted before breaking off the analysis. He came to see me again twenty years later, aged beyond measure and trembling with the Parkinson's disease he had been suffering from for some time. We talked about that last dream, and he told me he had understood that I was the only one who had tried to help him, even though for a long time he had hated me, and that he had come to see me because he had wanted to express his appreciation. He spoke to me at length of a woman he had lived with after breaking off the analysis, telling me he wanted to get back in touch with her, although many years had now passed. His story was filled with a pain that I hadn't seen in him before. He told me that they didn't want him to meet her again, that they had had made a protective circle around her that he had never managed to penetrate. Before saying goodbye he asked me, with sudden passion, if I could look for her, if I could telephone her to tell her he was looking for her, that he still wanted to see her and talk to her, that now he was ready to be close to her in a way he had not been in the past. I knew he would not be able to come back to see me because of the distance, and yet I told him that I would be able to talk about her with him, but I couldn't do more than that... I watched him leave disconsolate, feeling lonelier than ever. I remembered a young psychotic patient who had wandered around the city all night, looking for a girl whose face he had glimpsed in the crowd; I recalled his unbounded sorrow at not having met her again... I knew that Parkinson's disease could allow a hitherto latent psychosis to surface, and realized that this was exactly what had happened to my old patient.

This was confirmed to me some time later by a psychiatrist who had treated him in the far-off city where he now lived.

The magic circle—the same as the one of which Jung had spoken many years earlier—had protected him by keeping away the anima, its emotions, its anxieties, its needs, with their disruptive power; and now that the distance had perhaps become unbridgeable, any other suffering, even the one once most feared, had turned into this, into the emptiness left by the lost anima. This was the same threat that had brought into analysis the young musician, who from adolescence had fenced off his anxieties by identifying himself with personalized images of detachment and spiritual superiority, leading to affective isolation and paralysis of the imagination.

The process which I had the fortune to witness, and to some extent play a part in, brought about a noticeable change in this patient of mine, and not just an inner one, for he came to be able to teach serenely, distancing himself from his maestro and going back to composing music that had become more expressive of his feelings, more emotive than it had ever been before—'Puccinian' music in a way. Eventually he fell in love with a girl to whom he was at last bound by affection and sensual pleasure. He had slowly come down from that high and solitary place from which he had watched, with fear and impotent desire, life passing by at his feet, at a distance; and the descent had been a gradual lowering himself into the intimacy of his story and his emotions, and at the same time a getting closer to people and to things, something he had once shrunk from in fear as any form of intimacy was a threat to his difference, to his unstable sense of identity.

On one occasion that we returned to that dream of Pope John, now distant in time but still vivid in his memory, he told me that the way he felt about it had changed. The analogy with Michelangelo's fresco now seemed to him only superficial, and in reality too grandiose, too heroic: it did not correspond to the feeling that had made him think in the dream: 'If only I could touch him!' He told me that those words were the same as the ones that a poor, sick and humiliated woman had thought, in much the same way as he had in the dream, as Jesus passed her by, separated from her by the throng which huddled around him: 'If only I could touch his robe, I would be healed!' And in confirmation of the validity of this similarity, there was the rest of the Gospel story, in which Jesus had sensed the energy going out from him, and had asked 'who' had touched him. For it was not the undifferentiated contact of the crowd that had been able to liberate the healing power, but the one sought with humble faith by an individual, just as my patient had done in the dream—and thus a specific and differentiated relationship.

This new comment of his implied that a change had taken place, in particular the growth of the trust barely hinted at in the beginning, but immediately repressed; and it revealed the action of the dyad, the syzygy, in its form of healing spirit and wounded anima. In that trusting contact, in the meeting of humble request and free, generous response, was liberated a healing power that had previously been inhibited by the split state of the dyad; an inner recomposition induced by the analysis, which in the synergy of this dyad could perhaps recognize the image of both his own goal and his own essence.

Several years later, a similar descent, with the same meaning and comparable beneficent consequences, was shown and taught to me by two other patients, whose most significant dreams in this connection offered me further comment and amplification.

A woman, aged about thirty-five at the time, dreamed of being on a high tower, from which she looked out over the plain and the sea spread before her. She had the impression that the tower was in some way her own work, but above all that she had been up there too long, and the time had come to go down and get to know the people she saw swarming at her feet. Descending, she found herself among people whom she could now distinguish clearly, unlike before. Not that she liked them particularly; on the contrary. But being with them, she thought, was after all a natural thing; she felt at home; and then there was the nearby sea, into which she could plunge at last.

The dream of a man of the same age, engaged in classical studies, had a majestic, epic tone, and seemed not to be addressed to him alone. In other words it preserved a 'high' quality despite its contents, and this may have been why it took a long time for its meaning to begin to be really assimilated, and to find some parallel in the patient's life. In the dream, a man shut up in a small room, perhaps a cell, was writing an account of something that was taking place, which everybody knew about and whose outcome was anxiously awaited. As the man wrote about it, the dreamer watched the events unfold, and at the same time listened to the account: a cosmonaut was flying in his capsule, searching on behalf of all humanity for a life that filled the heavens; his face, now visible, was distorted by an expression of boundless grief. The words of the narrator were now a sorrowful chant, saying that the cosmonaut had not found any life in the heavens, that emptiness surrounded the Earth and human beings were alone. Then the people embraced one another in tears. Now they knew that nothing was left to them except taking care of the fragile, unique life that existed on Earth; for nothing would restore life to life that had been destroyed. The dreamer had woken up crying, feeling that he was both the man telling the story and the cosmonaut, as well as one of the waiting men. He then began to think that his weakness, his fear of living, was a necessary condition for the intimacy that he sought, and that it was no longer necessary for him to confine himself in a 'lofty' ideal of Self, for he would not win that intimacy through the admiration or desire stirred by a presumed height; on the contrary, it was precisely the feeling that something was missing which would be able to open him up to an encounter with other existences, and release him from his distressing isolation.

The descent of which I am speaking, as this last dream makes clear, possesses an intrinsic character of depression; or perhaps it would be better to call it melancholy. There is in fact a depression nurtured by the rejection of loss and of failure, steeped in angry resentment and guilt, which is rooted in an implicit pretension of wholeness: an offshoot of the autonomy and complexual hypertrophy of the ego, i.e. of its inflation by the Self. Melancholy, on the contrary, pervades the soul in the face of the transitoriness of beloved things. It is compassion for their finite nature: an emotional tone that accompanies the descent of the spirit from its eternal and distant world into the particulars of time. In its descent, in fact, the spirit recognizes the immutable destiny of death that marks every aspect of life, and it is precisely in the compassionate knowledge of death that it finds its fulfilment in time, for it entrusts to the transient, to the mortal, the feeling of eternity that is its specific characteristic. Thus, while removing any illusion of duration from the things of time, it reveals that the impermanent is a complete manifestation of being.

So melancholy pervades our soul at the moment of the union of spirit and anima, healing spirit and wounded anima, and out of this union is generated the process of individuation, at least as I understand it. Not a process of ascent—as it appears from the perspective of the Self when it is still an autonomous complex—which runs the risk at every step of feeding the illusion of wholeness and power; but a process of descent that is also an initiation into death, as can happen only when the link is strong with the particulars of the world that we are passing through, with the transitory things that we love, and which take at least part of us with them each time they disappear or die; a progressive rooting in Hades, the invisible god of the underworld for whom the soul is destined.

At that time, John W. Perry had not yet written the books that towards the end of the seventies introduced me to an understanding of those processes of renewal of the Self, which can produce a psychotic cataclysm in schizoid personalities. And I was not even aware of his revision of the theory of complexes—formulated in just those years—so in keeping with Hillman's contemporary polytheistic revision of psychology, with its related polycentric conception of the soul. Then I was studying the work of Ronald Fairbairn and even more that of Henry Guntrip, in order to get a better understanding of the schizoid state. In that state, argued Guntrip, an essential core of the psyche, perhaps its spiritual core, following a trauma that is usually chronic, withdraws into an unreachable elsewhere and is obliged to remain in that refuge outside life pending the return of conditions that would give it a more suitable reception (Guntrip 1968). An intuition very similar, it seemed to me, to the one to be found in some of Jung's stories, where that core was personified in a divine child, the incorruptible germ of the personality, hidden in a protected place and awaiting the propitious moment to descend into the world, or to return to the place from which it had just appeared.

At the time Guntrip used the expression 'parental complex' to indicate the set of these phenomena, distancing himself even in terminology from the Freudian tradition out of which he came. This interested me greatly, but what I found even more interesting was his masterly dramatization of that fundamental state, the individuation of the personalizations caused by dissociation—in particular by the dissociation that sadomasochistically contrasts 'masculine' with 'feminine', animus with anima—which was used to cope with the emergence of intolerable images. In addition to this, however, Guntrip confirmed the conviction I had received from Jung, that the decisive factor in treatment was not a technical, diagnostic or psychodynamic skill, a conceptualized understanding of the causes or models of relation and transference; and as a consequence, that this knowledge could not be central in the training of an analyst, because such knowledge, destined by its characteristics to be taken literally, could in the end collude precisely with the schizoid style of relationship with psychic reality that analysis set out to rectify.

For what was decisive to treatment instead was the establishment of a growing and basically stable intimacy with a 'good object', as Guntrip called it, of an empathic contact—at times, even if desired, greatly feared and a source of covert resistance—capable of liberating that flow of energy, i.e. that profound recognition which my patient's dream and the passage from the Gospels that he remembered represented in such a powerful way. For the good object is not so much the one that stirs sympathy or affection, but the one capable of an attentive relationship with the different aspects of the soul and with its individual manifestations: the images, the emotions, the personalizations that appear in the accounts of a life, or that are presented in the vicissitudes of transference. It is this personal contact, as Jung has so insistently underlined (CW 17, pars. 181 ff), which can open a breach in the closed structure of complexes, and restore to the whole of the psyche the energy that has been choked up in them. That is what happened in the dream to which I have returned several times. In the empathic contact, therefore, knowledge and relationship coincide: you don't get one without the other; and this is another way of describing the consciousness of syzygy, which permits such an improvement in understanding that Jung regarded it as specific to the psychotherapist and his action.

The importance to psychic life of the capacity for empathy was first pointed out by Edith Stein around 1917, in the years in which Jung was busy defining his own thinking about psychological types, the functions of consciousness and the imagination as a living synthesis of the different functions. What the two authors had in common was their concern to give a central place, in the body of psychological knowledge, to the perception of distinctiveness, or of the differences that define the individual in relation both to other individuals and to inner life. This was something that implied a value judgement on the traits of the personality, whether one's own or somebody else's. In other words, they shared a need to define the emergence and even the recognizable existence of particular qualities, and which mental faculty was entrusted with the task of attaining this end. Stein identified empathy as the capacity to realize the essential perception of individual and individuating differences, and argued that this is quite another thing from taking subjective experience, identification, as a measure (Stein 1917). The latter is in fact a mode of relationship that takes over when the capacity for empathy has been compromised and a Self has been constituted as an autonomous complex, drawing the ego upwards and away from that on which it is focused, on which it imposes its own experience as a truth.

I believe that empathy and imagination are the expression of one and the same form of consciousness—the consciousness of syzygy—

viewed from two different sides. And just as Stein distinguished empathy from identification, i.e. from emotional involvement, Jung made a distinction between true and false imagination: the former intent on recognizing the form of the different, the latter on reducing the different to forms subordinate to a domineering subjectivity.

Empathy is blocked or inhibited, sometimes very early on, when the empathic contact—whether extra- or intrapsychic—turns out to be too painful, unbearable. We can imagine, in this case, a dissociative process of syzygy that separates and opposes anima and animus, the spirit, and in the spirit goes so far as to break up the *senex/puer* dyad, whose synergy is needed to give form and feasibility to the possible. Perhaps this is why the divine child withdraws into its inaccessible refuges, and this absence renders the splitting of the syzygy permanent, making empathic contact impossible. This lack of empathy becomes in turn the decisive factor in those further splits, in those inner and outer antagonisms that result in the defensive strengthening of an ordering centre, the hypertrophy and autonomy of un complex, which in its defensive function tends to organize and contain the centrifugal fragments of the psyche in a rigid, constrictive order.

It could also be said that in this state the Old King, Kronos, the Senex, devours his children, preventing them from being born, from being exposed to the world, from giving rise to new and perhaps disturbing possibilities of life. So it is in the belly of Kronos, in the heart of his defensive mechanism, that we can find the divine child hidden; and the *filius*, finally set free, is what in fact forges the link that reunites the divided syzygy. From the synergy discovered or rediscovered in this way springs the empathy, or the imagination, that fertilizes and renews psychic life, and the dark impulse towards form can then find a way to be realized in the world, transforming the possible into a multiplicity of forms, into the long-awaited blooming of the *multi flores*.

It may be thought, therefore, that individuation starts to take place when, with a pervasive feeling of melancholy, the Self begins to dissolve as an autonomous complex; in other words when the drive to unify the multiple fades; and at the same time the capacity to discern and correlate differences, i.e. the capacity for empathy is gradually liberated. The consequent, complicated and articulate relations with the outer and inner world then appear as the expression of an original rediscovered possibility, of an unconditioned opening up to being. And so we do not have the definition of an identity, however complex, but on the contrary an endless un-defining.

Not the ideal *unicum*, as the centralizing action of the autonomous complex suggested, but if anything a *unitas multiplex*, expression of spirit and anima in dynamic synergy: a range of increasingly complex relations, multiple and different in space and time, a variety of interwoven stories, an inner and outer community, bound together by links that are forged by empathy, links of understanding and sympathy, of resemblance and difference, sometimes even of contrast and contradiction, if not downright aversion. And the stronger are those links and the deeper the memory, the more coherent and harmonious will be the cosmos that takes shape and the meaning that emanates from it; even if the whole, as Jung himself argued, will never be attained, and at most will offer a foretaste from time to time in the resplendent intensity of a fragment, turned into the 'empirical symbol' of its presence, and its centre, as a place which in that moment is home to a god.

I would like to sum up what has been said so far in a formula reminiscent of those of apophatic theology: 'That Self which is said to be the Self is not the Self but an idol to be shattered'. A point of view that also allows us to update the ancient *logos* of Thales, recorded by Plato (*Laws* 899 b) and Aristotle (*De anima* 411 a 7), 'all things are full of gods'. No longer speaking of gods, as we end up speaking of gods as of things; seeking instead to speak of things, of the events of this world and of the inner world, as if they were gods, i.e. as visible repositories of the invisible; with the reverence, the religious respect due to that singular way in which the invisible is made manifest, and letting the invisible show itself in the words that name things, in words from which the angel is set free. Things, in fact, like inner events, are particulars and invite us to leave the overall visions—theologies, mythologies, psychologies—at a distance, in the background, barely hinted at, but without denying them, since things and events include the perspectives from which they are encountered and considered; and in this the meeting of spirit and anima comes about. For the embrace of spirit and anima an inner space opens up, the intermediate space of the imagination, a crossroads at which the visible and the invisible meet and coexist, in the form of single things; where the fragments of time are composed in the memory, which in a manner independent of our intention is constructing a story, 'our' story.

To us, however, the flow of life looks like the back of a carpet while it is being woven, with knots, tangles and incomprehensible snarls. And it is only at the end—we sometimes think—that the front of the carpet will become visible, along with its pattern and its colours, perhaps beautiful and expressive in a way that could not be predicted. Then we imagine that a silent craftsman has skilfully woven the most disparate threads and the colours, designing the garden that the carpet will finally represent, the visible in which invisible things are occasionally revealed.

CHAPTER NINE

The Experience of Beauty

In August 1913, Sigmund Freud was on holiday with some friends at San Martino di Castrozza. One day, he recounts in a short piece written some time later, 'I went on a summer walk through a smiling countryside in the company of a taciturn friend and of a young but already famous poet. The poet admired the beauty of the scene around us but felt no joy in it. He was disturbed by the thought that all this beauty was fated to extinction, that it would vanish when winter came, like all human beauty and all the beauty and splendour that men have created or may create. All that he would otherwise have loved and admired seemed to him to be shorn of its worth by the transience which was its doom' (Freud 1916a, p.305).

Beauty and Transience. These are the opening words of *On Transience,* a little masterpiece just three pages long published in 1915, in which his thoughts are prompted by the observations made on that walk: 'The proneness to decay of all that is beautiful and perfect can, as we know, give rise to two different impulses in the mind. The one leads to the aching despondency felt by the young poet, while the other leads to rebellion against the fact asserted' (Freud 1916a, p.305). A third impulse of the mind, to which the following reflections will introduce us little by little, is the one that Freud will invite us to understand and foster.

These are pages unusually pervaded with melancholy, for Freud. They lack the detachment that generally goes hand in hand with his limpid prose; and they lead us to think that for him these reflections were a way of giving voice and meaning, *logos*, to the profound pathos that occupied his mind in those days, reawakened and kept alive by inescapable historical circumstances: by the imminent and now certain separation from Jung at the time he began to think them, by the war when he wrote them. A confirmation of this seems to come, among the writings of what was moreover a very fertile year for Freud, from the last of his metapsychological essays, *Mourning and Melancholia*, and from the *Thoughts for the Times on War and Death*. Yet none of these writings communicates the same intensity of gloomy pathos: I believe that this is because what is missing from them, or is only hinted at in the background, is the juxtaposition of beauty and transience that opens and underpins these three wonderful pages.

In vain, he goes on, he sought to persuade his two friends that the transience of what is beautiful does not imply any loss of its worth; on the contrary, its value increases with its scarcity, in part because this preserves it from fading as a result of familiarity and easy availability: 'The beauty of the human form and face vanish for ever in the course of our own lives, but their evanescence only lends them a fresh charm. A flower that blossoms only for a single night does not seem to us on that account less lovely'. And then, with an almost imperceptible shift in his reasoning, but one that is already hinted at in this passage, he changes the focus from the thing that looks beautiful and is there for aesthetic enjoyment to the person who experiences this enjoyment: '... the value of all this beauty and perfection is determined only by its significance for our own emotional lives, it has no need to survive us and is therefore independent of absolute duration' (Freud 1916a, pp.305-306). An argument that seemed conclusive to him, but not to his friends, so stubborn in their desire for the eternal duration of what had seduced them with its beauty, and in their bitterness over its decay, fading, disappearance.

And yet in that very argument lay the decisive difference between him and them: his detachment from beautiful things, which kept alive his sensitivity to beauty everywhere, and to its constant renewal, and their attachment, which jeopardized the experience of beauty itself. 'What spoilt their enjoyment of beauty must have been a revolt in their minds against mourning. The idea that all this beauty was transient was giving these two sensitive minds a foretaste of mourning over its decease; and, since the mind instinctively recoils from anything that is painful, they felt their enjoyment of beauty interfered with by thoughts of its transience' Freud 1916a, p.306). And so they ended up resisting the experience of beauty itself, once they had understood that it brought with it, inevitably, the experience of transience and mourning inherent in it.

Not that Freud was able to go beyond this consideration, even though he perceived in himself the different frame of mind of someone who had by now surrendered to that mourning, sufficiently at least to no longer put up a rebellion as obstinate as it was ineffective. In fact he was unable to explain why the detachment from objects we love is always so painful: 'We only see that libido clings to its objects and will not renounce those that are lost even when a substitute lies ready to hand'. Yet he knew—and perhaps it was in this experience, understood and appreciated, that his difference from his friends was rooted—that mourning, however painful it may be, comes to an end, and that letting go of what is lost leaves the libido free 'to replace the lost objects by fresh ones equally or still more precious'. This was true even for the terrible experience which in that moment he shared not just with his companions of that summer, but with other Europeans caught up in the destruction of the war: 'When once the mourning is over, it will be found that our high opinion of the riches of civilization has lost nothing from our discovery of their fragility. We shall build up again all that war has destroyed, and perhaps on firmer ground and more lastingly than before' (Freud 1916a, pp.306-307). A touching act of faith, this, in the soul's capacity to descend into the underworld, cross the dark waters of the Acheron and climb back up to the light again, purified of earlier ties and open to a new life; but only if it has truly been able to confront death, bringing the ego into the underworld with it: an ego that is so often obstinate in clinging to its identity and attachments, and unwilling to let go of the grip on the reality with which it is familiar, even when that reality has in fact vanished.

We can read this short essay as Freud's evocation, from his own perspective, of the archetypal experience that Jung described in writings like *On Rebirth.* Above all, however, it is interesting for the complex vision that he shows himself to have of the aesthetic experience, that of an inextricable blend of enthusiasm and sadness, of a gleam of eternity that emerges from the shadow of death. A disturbing experience, therefore, that accounts, among other things, for the anxieties which accompany any attempt to represent it, especially, but not solely, through the forms of poetry and the arts.

In those very years, in a less troubled part of Europe, Fernando Pessoa encountered a new heteronym: 'Doctor Ricardo Reis was born in my soul on 29 January 1914, around 11 in the evening'. Like Alberto Caeiro, Álvaro de Campos, Bernardo Soares and yet others, Reis was one particular personification of Pessoa's soul, a *daimon*, like Jung's Philemon, who also appeared on the scene in those years. Reis's imagination took on forms of its own, followed its own paths: he was a doctor, with a great respect for science, and the poet to whom Pessoa entrusted his own 'mental discipline, cloaked in the music that is peculiar to him' (Pessoa 1984, p.19). Through Reis, a neoclassical theory, dreamed up one evening in reaction to the excesses of modernism, was transformed into poems where beauty and transience are interwoven in crystalline verses that seem to have no other theme. And Lydia was the woman to whom most of those verses were addressed, at least in appearance, as she was in reality the image of the anima that generated them. Or rather, they were generated by the intimacy of the conversation that Reis had with her, the fact of being in *syzygy* with her; and we can imagine them, those verses, as they flow from their mutual gazes, from the melancholic smile that one exchanged with the other.

Reis was an epicurean poet like Horace, from whom he took his inspiration, and he would have found Freud's brief essay, if he had ever read it, congenial. There was no trace of rebellion against impermanence in him. On the contrary, it seems that impermanence was the background against which beauty made its appearance to him, a beauty that his soul reflected meekly, but without hanging onto it.

> The gods grant nothing more than life,
> So let us reject whatever lifts us
>   To unbreathable heights,
>   Eternal but flowerless.
> All that we need to accept is science,
> And as long as the blood in our veins still pulses
>   And love does not shrivel,
>   Let us go on
> Like panes of glass: transparent to light,
> Pattered by the sad rain trickling down,
>   Warmed by the sun,
>   And reflecting a little.[1]

Above all it could be said that it was precisely the refinement of his sensibility in the daily trial of decay and loss that made possible for Reis the experience of beauty, at the moment in which it is revealed before fading away. And this, only this, was for him the eternity granted to human beings, but a present and tangible one.

It is so sweet the flight of this day,
Lydia, which we do not seem to be living.
Without doubts the gods
are grateful to us in this hour,

noble compensation this faith of ours
in the exiled truth of their bodies
they give us the high reward
of letting us be

lucid companions of their calm,
heirs for a moment of their skill
at living the whole of life
in a single moment,

a single moment, Lydia, in which separated
from earthly troubles we receive
Olympian delights
in our souls.

And for a single moment we feel ourselves
immortal gods for the calm that we wear
and the haughty indifference
to fleeting things.

Like those who hold on to the crown of victory
these faded laurels of a single day
we preserve to be proud of,
in the wrinkled future,

perpetually in our view the certain proof
that the gods one moment loved us
and gave us an hour
not ours, but of Olympus.[2]

Reis's poems appeared in large numbers throughout 1914, growing less frequent in later years but continuing right up to the last year of Pessoa's life, 1935. The presence of the doctor poet in his mind was not a literary device. His independent and intense voice rose from the depths of a 'partial personality', as Jung would have called it, and this accounted for the constancy of the themes and of the tone in which they were couched. This is something that we see when we look at any of the other 'personalities' that inhabited Pessoa's mind.

Reis was in love with beauty, and allowed the pain of its loss to pass through him without rejecting it, and without turning against the beauty in objects that remained available; thus he didn't miss the experience, and the seed of eternity in which beauty lies was not wanting. He could entrust to poetry, to the process through which it emerged as well as the verses themselves, the quiet testimony of that experience and of the regeneration that stemmed from it. For the experience of beauty constitutes the solid foundation of an existence, as is suggested by another of Reis's odes, the first of the few which Pessoa published in his lifetime.

> Safe I sit on the solid pillar
>   of the verses in which I persist,
> nor do I fear the numberless future influence
>   of the times and of forgetfulness;
> so that if the mind, absorbed, contemplates in itself
>   the reflections of the world,
> it makes lifeblood of them, and creates in art
>   the world that resembles itself.
> Thus on stone the external instant carves
>   its own being, and there lasts.[3]

Like Freud, Reis had shifted the focus of his attention from the things in which beauty manifests itself to the mind which recognizes and contemplates that beauty, and whose state becomes essential to the very possibility of the aesthetic experience. Moreover, he had seen in art the only process in which 'the external instant' can leave a lasting sign. Following the classical spirit, he entrusted art with the task of giving perpetual form to the 'reflections of the world', and to their beauty, as if carving them on stone; and for him this was the eternity granted to mortals, a permanent dwelling in which mortals can live with trust.

Stone as a metaphor is charged with ancient powers. This is clear from the teaching of Giovanni Semerano, who traces it back to the Akkadian *di'u, tu,* which means 'stela', 'pedestal in the temple', 'stone', and the Greek term *theos*, 'god' (Semerano 2004, p.105). He also points out that the *theos* of Thales, as handed down by Aristotle, evoked the soul of the cosmos infused 'even in the stone of Magnesia' (*De anima* I, 2). Even with the choice of this metaphor, therefore, Reis recognized in poetry the divine in which the fragile events of the world find substance, and in which poetry itself finds sense and necessity, as Hölderlin had already suggested in his memorable line: 'poetically, man dwells on this earth'.[4]

The 'emotional lives' of which Freud had spoken and 'the mind, absorbed, [that] contemplates in itself / the reflections of the world', of Reis's ode are different names for the imagination. It is in the imagination that the experience of transience becomes aesthetic experience, and this is possible because the imagination is a form of weak understanding that does not evade impermanence but participates in it; indeed, it is rooted in it—in part because *phantasia* is indissolubly linked with bodily sensation, as Aristotle thought (*De anima* I, 1). For this reason the imagination meets the same fate as transience, in the view of those who, to escape it, reject 'whatever lifts us / To unbreathable heights, / Eternal but flowerless'; losing, however, the fragile charm of Aphrodite *iostephanou*, 'wreathed in violets', for whom the Homeric hymns dedicated to her reserved a dual epithet: *glukumeilike*, 'sweetly smiling', and *philommeides*, 'smile loving'—smile that raises a sweet smile.

There is an experience of beauty that does not occur in places outside us, or through the medium of poetic expression, but in regions of the mind that are hard to reach—its nether regions we might call them—into which we happen to descend, or sometimes plunge, especially when the identity on which we have relied disintegrates, revealing its deep-seated fragility or its character of a now obsolete defensive structure. Jung gives an example of this in the chapter of the *Memories* in which he recounts his 'confrontation with the unconscious', an encounter that unfolds as a journey of initiation into this rare and yet essential experience of beauty.

These were the same years in which Freud conceived and then wrote *On Transience*, and Pessoa encountered the doctor poet Reis in his soul. A fantasy and a dream of December 1913, in fact, marked the initial stage of this process, which takes place in the 'dark depths'—and the words 'dark' and 'darkness' are the ones that occur most often in the account—until there appears the uncertain light of a dawn, the first rays of the newborn sun, when the vision approaches its dramatic end and the new light emerges to illuminate a fatal event.

From the presentiment in the fantasy to the conclusion in the dream, we follow with Jung the final trajectory of a hero, who intends to assert his will with overwhelming force, and instead goes to meet his destiny of death: '... the attitude embodied by Siegfried, the hero, no longer suited me. Therefore it had to be killed.... After the deed I felt an overpowering compassion, as though I myself had been shot: a sign of my secret identity with Siegfried, as well as the grief man feels when he is forced to sacrifice his ideal and his conscious attitudes. This identity and my heroic idealism had to be abandoned, for there are higher things than the ego's will, and to these one must bow (Jung 1963, p.205).

Jung was thirty-eight at the time: at the beginning of the year, on 6 January, he had said farewell to Freud in a letter, and the break was made official in September, at the Fourth International Psychoanalytical Congress in Munich. Jung was undergoing a profound agitation in his mind, a rapid erosion of his habitual and settled state by 'an incessant stream of fantasies', whose extraneous and disturbing character he found bewildering. Henri Ellenberger (1970) would use the words 'creative illness' to describe this commotion, in which one form of existence began to die, leaving room for a new orientation that burst in with force but was still incomprehensible—one could also speak, I believe, of a tumultuous 'restructuring of the Self', but not so violent as to prevent a gradual assimilation and transformation of the impetuous phenomena in the mind. 'To the extent that I managed to translate the emotions into images', comments Jung in fact, 'that is to say, to find the images which were concealed in the emotions—I was inwardly calmed and reassured. Had I left those images hidden in the emotions, I might have been torn to pieces by them.' (Jung 1963, p. 201). It proved necessary, in order for this to happen, not to treat the contents as absolutely extraneous; however, he recalls, 'one of the greatest difficulties for me lay in dealing with my negative feelings: I was voluntarily submitting myself to emotions of which I could not really approve, and I was writing down fantasies which often struck me as nonsense, and toward which I had strong resistances.... In order to grasp the fantasies which were stirring in me "underground", I knew that I had to let myself plummet down into them, as it were. I felt not only violent resistance to this, but a distinct fear.' (Jung 1963, p. 202). This rebellion was probably a hangover from the heroic attitude, not yet entirely vanished; or, in other words, it was due to the persistence of a hypertrophy of the intellectual and volitional components of the ego, along with their ideals, at the expense of the imaginal component, still to some degree subject to inhibition, and thus prevented from emerging freely and assuming control of the ego complex at this juncture.

This first phase, in which destruction, disorientation and the fear of becoming fragmented and lost prevailed, and emotions and images arose in a confused muddle (at least as far as we can tell from Jung's account), was followed by a different experience, which finally saw the imaginal ego guiding the process. Jung began to descend deliberately into what he later described as a land of the dead. Commenting on this as an old man, he would say that the relationship with the unconscious 'is also a relationship to the collectivity of the dead, for the unconscious corresponds to the mythic land of the dead, the land of the ancestors'; thus, when the mind withdraws into the unconscious, and this was what had happened to him in those years, 'it produces a mysterious animation and gives visible form to the ancestral traces, the collective contents. Like a medium, it gives the dead a chance to manifest themselves' and to become 'the voices of the Unanswered, Unresolved, and Unredeemed' (Jung 1963, p.216), that call out and ask questions from the inner world.

In the realm of the dead he met imaginal presences with which he could by now establish a living relationship in time: the first were Elijah and Salome, who reassembled in him the *syzygy*—'Elijah', recounts Jung, 'assured me that he and Salome had belonged together from all eternity' (Jung 1963, p.206), even though he was an old man and she a young girl.

It is precisely the presence of Elijah and Salome that renders more obvious an omission from the *Memories* that was certainly due to discretion, but which would have deprived us of an essential piece of information if Barbara Hannah had not filled the gap in her biography of Jung: the part that was played, as friendly companion in his confrontation with the unconscious, by Toni Wolff, thirteen years younger than him, but above all as much *puella*, as a psychological type, as Jung, who had been nicknamed 'Father Abraham' at school, was *senex*. This was the crucible in which the *syzygy* was reforged and appeared in the semblance of the Elijah-Salome couple; it was in the closeness of this relationship that his love of images was reawakened, and with it the ability to feel loved and not threatened by them. Jung was no longer a solitary hero—Siegfried really was dead—and now it was not just intellect and will that sustained him, but trust in the imagination as well, as can only happen in a warmed heart. And even the attitude of responsibility towards images, on which Jung so insisted, was indeed supported by the will and clarified by the intellect but, like that towards people, found its roots and sap in love.

After Elijah and Salome came Philemon, who 'was a pagan and brought with him an Egypto-Hellenistic atmosphere with a Gnostic coloration' (Jung 1963, p.207) and appeared to be an evolution of Elijah. We can even see Philemon in a drawing in a manuscript dating from those years, on page 154 of the *Red Book*, written by Jung in 1916: he appears as an old man with a white beard, his gaze directed straight ahead, his wings outspread against a blue, twilight sky.

154

Ich gehe meine strasse weiter, ein feingeschliffen, in zehn feuern gehärtet stahl, im gewande geborg. mein begleiter ein panzerhemd liegt mir um die brust heimlich unter dem mantel getragen. über nacht gewann ich die schlange lieb, ich habe ihr rätsel erraten. ich setze mich zu ihnen auf die heissen steine am wege. ich weiss sie listig und grausam zu fangen, jene kalten teufel, die dem ahnungslosen in die ferse stechen. ich bin ihr freund geworden und blase ihnen eine mildtönende flöte. meine höhle aber schmücke ich mit ihren schillernden häuten. wie ich so meines weges dahinschritt, da kam ich zu einem rötlichen felsen, darauf lag eine grosse buntschillernde schlange. da ich nun beim grossen ΦΙΛΗΜΩΝ die magie gelernt hatte, so holte ich meine flöte hervor und blies ihr ein süsses zauberlied vor, dass sie glauben machte, sie sei meine seele. als sie genügend bezaubert war, ...

Philemon, in the Red Book, 1916

An image of particular intensity, as are the others painted or sculpted later on by Jung, who displayed great ability in 'giving form' to his fantasies—*Gestalten* was a word of which he was very fond and used widely, points out Christian Gaillard in a fine book devoted to Jung's 'imaginary museum' (1998). And what Jung wrote about Philemon, with whom he had a long relationship, allows us to understand clearly what he himself had attained on this stage of his journey of initiation:

> Philemon and other figures of my fantasies brought home to me the crucial insight that there are things in the psyche which I do not produce, but which produce themselves and have their own life. Philemon represented a force which was not myself. In my fantasies I held conversations with him, and he said things which I had not consciously thought. For I observed clearly that it was he who spoke, not I. He said I treated thoughts as if I generated them myself, but in his view thoughts were like animals in the forest, or people in a room, or birds in the air, and added, "If you should see people in a room, you would not think that you made these people, or that you were responsible for them." It was he who taught me psychic objectivity, the reality of the psyche. Through him the distinction was clarified between myself and the object of my thought. He confronted me in an objective manner, and I understood that there is something in me which can say things that I do not know and do not intend, things which may even be directed against me. Psychologically, Philemon represented superior insight. He was a mysterious figure to me. At times he seemed to me quite real, as if he were a living personality. I went walking up and down the garden with him, and to me he was what the Indians call a guru. (Jung 1963, pp.207-8).

Jung tried to 'formulate and express what might have been said by Philemon' (Jung 1963, pp.214-15) in the *VII Sermones ad Mortuos*, which he then transcribed in the *Red Book* in elegant Gothic letters, suited to its peculiar language. In the *Red Book* he had attempted, by his own admission, an aesthetic working-through of his fantasies, but this step, while proving necessary, could not be the conclusive one; for him, stopping at that point would have been an 'aestheticizing' lapse, to use his expression. It was not yet the right language to represent his experience: 'I saw', he comments, 'that so much fantasy needed firm ground underfoot, and that I must first return wholly to reality. For me, reality meant scientific comprehension. I had to draw concrete conclusions from the insights the unconscious had given me—and that task was to become a life work (MDR, p.213).

Jung observed that language, however accurate, could not be a substitute for life; if it tried to replace it, not only did life lose vigour, but it impoverished itself. Language is a bridge, and its precision, its aesthetic refinement, its ability to excite inner resonances, are necessary to link the two worlds, not to replace one of them; and this is particularly true of the language of psychology. For the same reason, it should not be forgotten that when the aesthetic sensibility is inhibited, and the action of the imaginal ego is inhibited, images slip away, and with the images a real relationship, an 'animate' relationship, with both the inner and the outer world.

In his *Memories* Jung tells how he had been tempted to consider himself an artist, and to regard the experience he had had of images as art. His resistance to this temptation was not due to a belittlement of the aesthetic experience, as has sometimes been claimed, but to the fact that establishing a connection between art—or 'creativity', as some might put it today—and his aesthetic experience, the practice of active imagination, would have meant lowering its value, by limiting it to an exceptional personality and a specific experience, it too exceptional; whereas he was convinced that it was significant because it pertained to all human beings, and more specifically to the suffering soul. Understanding and communicating this was the task he faced, and the language of science was the most effective tool at his disposal, and therefore in his view the best suited to the purpose.

Imagination, as Jung practiced it, was not aimed at the literal creation of a work, but at 'letting happen' a process that was in itself spontaneous, that had as its aim the metamorphosis of an existence: 'The art of letting things happen [*geschehenlassen*], action through non-action, letting go of oneself, as taught by Meister Eckhart, became for me the key opening the door to the way. *We must be able to let things happen in the psyche*. For us (in the West), this actually is an art of which few people know anything' (Jung 1967, par. 20), he wrote in a fundamental passage of his commentary on *The Secret of the Golden Flower*. This was the art of which he had become a master and which he has handed down, and by virtue of which he had been able to understand that the contents of the unconscious always possess a certain degree of autonomy in every human being and not just in the artist. He had also understood that it is difficult, but possible and necessary for the individual and for the psychotherapist, 'to accept the very fact of the autonomy of the unconscious' (Jung 1963, p.211), for it is on this acceptance that is based the possibility of an encounter which is in the end healing and not destructive. Thus the idea of the autonomy of the unconscious, of its spontaneous processes of change and of the ways of understanding it and helping it along without being swept away by it became, from that time on, the central and distinctive core of his psychological thinking.

Over the following years, judging by what Jung wrote about it, the process continued without the initial tumult, just as happens with the mountain torrent that subsides in the plain and turns into a slow and dignified river. Already in 1916, the year in which he composed the *Red Book*, with a keen aesthetic sensibility, Jung wrote *The Structure of the Unconscious*, the text of a lecture that would be included in the first part of *The Relations between the Ego and the Unconscious* in 1928, and a short essay that was not published until 1957, 'The Transcendent Function': in these writings he finally reconstructed, with a 'scientific' spirit and using 'scientific' metaphors, the inner experience of those years, laying a new foundation for his subsequent research.

This undertaking, to find an orderly structure of thought for his experience, which in the years immediately afterwards continued in his imposing work on psychological types, was accompanied by, or rather interwoven with, the exercise of the mandala, which he carried on with until 1928. He had painted his first mandala in 1916, after writing the *VII Sermones ad Mortuos*, without being aware of what it was or understanding its meaning. It was not until 1918-19, he relates, that he began to comprehend the function of these drawings, which had become a common practice for him:

> ... I sketched every morning in the notebook a small circular drawing, a mandala, which seemed to correspond to my inner situation at the time. With the hope of these drawings I could observe my psychic transformations from day to day.... To be sure, at first I could only dimly understand them; but they seemed to me highly significant, and I guarded them like precious pearls. I had the distinct feeling that they were something central .... When I began drawing the mandalas, however, I saw that everything, all the paths I had been following, all the steps I had taken, were leading back to a single point—namely, to the mid-point. It became increasingly plain to me that the mandala is the centre. ... Uniform development exists, at most, only at the beginning; later, everything points toward the centre. This insight gave me stability, and gradually my inner peace returned (Jung 1963, pp.20-22).

The mandala is the representation of a microcosm, and the soul is this microcosm. Losing the centre causes disorientation because the perception of an ordered microcosm is dependent on the perception of a centre around which everything is laid out: like the square of a town, to and from which all the streets run, a point of reference necessary to establish distances and relationships; or like a public building that soars above the others, to which we turn every time we are afraid of having lost our way, or to which the community flocks from every side, in order to take decisions together that are going to have an effect on all of them.

Greek mythology recognized this centre in the virgin goddess Hestia, whose name is thought to derive from *ousian* or *essian*, 'essence' (Plato, *Cratylus*, 401c-d), i.e., 'she that is', the being that founds. Symbol and pledge of stability, of immutability, of permanence and inviolability, Hestia stayed behind to look after the home of the gods when they joined Zeus in the cosmic procession (Plato, *Phaedrus*, 247a); and she was, like Vesta, the burning and sacred heart of the city of Rome, and for the family the safe hearth which, circular, central and fixed to the ground, rooted the dwelling in the earth.

This intense experience of a centre, around which and towards which the movements of the soul gravitated, was the germ from which the idea of the Self was born in Jung, and with it the conviction of having reached the place for which he was destined: 'I knew that in finding the mandala as an expression of the Self I had attained what was for me the ultimate' (Jung 1963, p.222).

The work that he was writing in those years, *Psychological Types*, itself appears, if we look closely at the structure that was being created, to be the equivalent of a mandala, a circle divided into four, a circumambulation around a centre, the Self. Once again the aesthetic experience was for Jung the bridge that allowed his exacting reason to represent what he had discovered through images in theoretical form. However, he wrote nothing explicitly on the mandala and its significance before the commentary on *The Secret of the Golden Flower*—a treatise on Taoist alchemy he received from its translator Richard Wilhelm, as he himself relates, in 1928, just when he was painting what was to be his last mandala.

In a short article of no more than three pages, written many years later, in 1955, Jung summed up the meaning of the spontaneous appearance of a mandala, which he had recognized 'in conditions of psychic dissociation or disorientation, for instance … as the result of a neurosis and its treatment... in schizophrenics whose view of the world has become confused, owing to the invasion of incomprehensible contents from the unconscious.' In all these cases 'it is easy to see how the severe pattern imposed by a circular image of this kind compensates the disorder and confusion of the psychic state—namely, through the construction of a central point to which everything is related, or by a concentric arrangement of the disordered multiplicity and of contradictory and irreconcilable elements' (Jung 1959, par. 387). An imaginative response to the state of suffering, an archetypal defence against fragmentation and violation, but one which to be truly effective, and above all to go beyond the function of mere defence and turn instead into goal and achievement, requires—as we have seen happened to Jung—the reconstitution of the *syzygy*, with the consequent restoration of the imaginal ego to its activity of mediation.

The Castle, Mandala at Vauban, 1928

But let us go back to 1927, the year in which Jung had a dream he considered decisive, because in it the goal of this long initiation was at last made entirely manifest; a goal that could not truly be understood, however, unless sufficient importance was given to the intense aesthetic experience through which its attainment was revealed.

Jung found himself along with some other Swiss people in a 'dark, sooty city', Liverpool, 'the pool of life' ('liver', as the symbolic seat of life), and climbed up from the harbour towards the hills on which the city lay.

> When we reached the plateau, we found a broad square, dimly illuminated by street lights, into which many streets converged. The various quarters of the city were arranged radially around the square. In the centre was a round pool, and in the middle of it, a small island. (The individual quarters of the city were also laid out radially around a central point represented by a small open square, lit by a larger lamppost, which was a small-scale replica of the island.) While everything around was obscured by rain, fog, smoke and dimly lit darkness, the little island blazed with sunlight. On it stood a single tree, a magnolia, in a sea of reddish blossoms. It was as though the tree stood in the sunlight and was, at the same time, the source of light. My companions commented on the abominable weather, and obviously did not see the tree. They spoke of another Swiss who was living in Liverpool, and expressed surprise that he should have settled here. I was carried away by the beauty [*schönheit*] of the tree and the sunlit island, and thought, I know very well why he has settled here. Then I awoke.' And he commented: '... I had had a vision of unearthly beauty [*überirdische schönheit*], and that was why I was able to live at all.... I had known, to be sure, that I was occupied with something important, but I still lacked understanding.... The clarification brought about by the dream made it possible for me to take an objective view of the things that filled my being (Jung 1963 pp.223-24).

His companions neither saw nor understood, or rather, they stopped at the dirt, at the soot, at the rain, at the dark of the night ('*in stercore vili invenitur lapis philosophorum*', 'in the dirt we will find the philosopher's stone': Jung 1953, par. 421), for in this case too the experience of beauty has an ambiguous, disturbing, dark context, which can mislead those who do not have eyes sensitive enough not to exclude anything, neither darkness nor light. And this dream is also able to tell us that we are living in a time in which the light lies repressed in the shadows, and that it is the vision of the light that escapes us, not the darkness that cloaks and conceals it.

Readers of this dream, like Jung's companions, can hide the vision of the truth from themselves by stopping at the 'symbols' (the island, the tree at the centre of the island, the lamppost that illuminates the individual squares, the at once central and polycentric structure of the city), thereby reducing the living experience of the dream to a 'sign', and precisely while it speaks of 'symbol'. Jung, though, was here a witness to the absolute, 'unearthly' (*überirdische*) beauty of the centre, of the Self, and it was this beauty that now filled his being and allowed him to live. The shining of beauty—*splendor formae*—is in fact the self-revelation of the fullness of being in a fragment of it, in this case the Self, and gives rise to a mystical experience, as Plato and Plotinus had understood before him: a shining that is also a vision of truth, the unveiling of the eternal eternally present in time. So Jung's experience can only be defined as 'mystical'. (Here I am following Henry Corbin, for whom *mystikos* is what is hidden and related to mystery, and therefore eludes perception by the senses, and the mystical experience stems from the penetration into the world of mystery, the 'country of the soul', where relationships of distance in space are replaced by relationships of distance between internally experienced states. Penetrating mystically into this country is possible through the organs of penetration, which are called 'inner vision', 'light of the heart' and 'active imagination', and are not exclusive to anyone, but atrophied in the majority (Corbin 1973, p.27). Jung's confrontation with the unconscious appears, as the Liverpool dream shows in three-dimensional form, to be a progressive penetration into the 'country of the soul' through the active imagination).

And what is more, any experience of the archetypal images with which the Self occasionally manifests itself in time, in the existence of the individual, cannot but be mystical; naturally in someone who has a lover's heart, as Plotinus put it, and is initiated to the vision and comprehension of beauty—in the dream, Jung's companions see nothing of what leaves him ecstatic... Here it seems as if Jung has followed the suggestion that Plotinus made in the sixth tractate of his *First Ennead*, devoted to beauty: 'Go back into yourself and look; and if you do not yet see yourself beautiful, then, just as someone making a statue which has to be beautiful cuts away here and polishes there and makes one part smooth and clears another till he has given his statue a beautiful face, so you too must cut away excess and straighten the crooked and clear the dark and make it bright and never stop... But if anyone comes to the sight blear-eyed with wickedness, and unpurified, or weak and by his cowardice unable to look at what is very bright, he sees nothing, even if someone shows him what is there and possible to see. For one must come to the sight with a seeing power made akin and like to what is seen.... [Never] can a soul see beauty without becoming beautiful' (*Enneads* I 6, 9)

All this is confirmed, if there were any need, by the enthusiastic words that Jung wrote ten years later, this time commenting on his vision of a work of architecture, the Taj Mahal, the mausoleum built in Agra by the Mogul Shah Jahan in memory of the young wife he had lost. This building, which he had seen during his visit to India in 1938, had made the spiritual yearning of the 'ancient Moguls', their erotic mysticism, even more evident and congenial to him than had their 'pure and beautiful' mosques: 'There is not much mind about it, but a great deal of feeling. …It is a desire, an ardent longing and even greed for God…the most poetic, most exquisite love of beauty'. And he continued:

> In a world of tyranny and cruelty, a heavenly dream crystallized in stone: the Taj Mahal. I cannot conceal my unmitigated admiration for this supreme flower, for this jewel beyond price, and I marvel at that love which discovered the genius of Shah Jehan and used it as an instrument of self-realization. This is the one place in the world where the—alas—all too invisible and all too jealously guarded beauty of the Islamic Eros has been revealed by a well-nigh divine miracle. It is the delicate secret of the rose gardens of Shiraz and of the silent patios of Arabian palaces, torn out of the heart of a great lover by a cruel and incurable loss. The mosques of the Moguls and their tombs may be pure and austere, their *divans*, or audience halls, may be of impeccable beauty, but the Taj Mahal is a revelation. …It is Eros in its purest form; there is nothing mysterious, nothing symbolic about it. It is the sublime expression of human love for a human being (Jung 1939b, par. 990).

Again the deeply felt experience of transience, the 'cruel and incurable loss', sadness as a necessary passage to a radical experience of beauty, which reaches to its foundation and is therefore transforming, capable of generating 'self-realization':: in a word, 'mystical'.

The beauty of the centre awakens and draws Eros to itself, and Eros circulates between the particular centres of the soul that reflect the beauty of the common centre, to which they are thereby kept spellbound. For this reason the experience of beauty has the power to reunite soul, to put it back together in a harmonious way, and from it comes the feeling of an intensity of life, of an existence rooted in a centre on which everything gravitates. Not that it was possible for Jung, or for anyone else, to stay in the centre, i.e. to expose himself continually to this vision of beauty: the awakening from the dream, immediately after the vision, tells us that that experience went beyond his emotional limits—and for this very reason could also be described as 'sublime'—and so had to be reduced to a brief moment, even though one present in the memory, and forever. Yet it would have been possible to remain close to the centre, where one does not see but knows and is attracted: this was what 'the other Swiss' did, and something that Jung could well understand.

Perhaps the condition permitted to mortals is to live in one or the other centre, to pass from one quarter of the soul to another, and find in each, as in a mirror, a similar light, a reflection, one might say, of the original light that constitutes the centre of centres and gives to it, and only to it, an absolute, sublime beauty. But a light that we can find again, albeit only reflected, in the centres 'transparent to light ... / and reflecting a little' where it is given to us to live. This is why it is said: '... poetically, man dwells on this earth'; because it is in the reflections of that 'unearthly', transcendent beauty that man recognizes the forms in which to erect his own dwelling, to house the gift of 'one moment', of 'an hour / not ours, but of Olympus', and finally, even if temporarily, to be admitted to peace in the fullness of his own being; it is in that 'doing' (*poiein*) in which poetry (*poiesis*) consists, which is not just the work of the poet, because *poiesis* is the very 'making' of Eros, which in beauty incessantly generates forms (*Gestalten*) of existence that are transient, ephemeral and nonetheless lovable.

[1] 'The gods grant nothing more than life' (Não consentem os deuses mais que a vida') in Pessoa 1998).

[2] 'It is so sweet the flight of this day' (È tão suave a fuga d'este dia') in F. Pessoa, *Livro do desassossego*. Translated from the Italian, 'È tanto suave la fuga di questo giorno' in F. Pessoa 2005, p. 227.

[3] 'Safe I sit on the solid pillar' ('Seguro assento na coluna firme'). Translated from the Italian, 'Sicuro siedo sulla colonna salda', in Pessoa 2005, p. 9.

[4] Holderlin, 'In lovely blueness...', Holderlin 2004, p.789..

APPENDIX I

The Care of Art

The body of western art is sorely afflicted by the loss of a sense of beauty and thereby of symbolic function. This state of suffering does not differ from what we find in the individual soul. The immanent idealism of modern consciousness has subjected both art and the individual soul to the general dominion of Father Time, Cronos, the father who devours his own children and imprisons in time every work born in time. Both have been separated from the original cult of Mnemosyne, the mother of the Muses, or memory, which connects the phenomena of time to their archetypal source. Once that source and even the memory of it have been lost, beauty too has been deprived of its true value, which is to symbolise time and eternity, rendering visible what is invisible in an image. Once it has been reduced by that immanentism to the position of a mere accidental attribute of things, beauty has left soul and art bewildered, as if condemned to exile in a one-dimensional land.

The feeling which arises in a state of exile is expressed by the word 'nostalgia', a term evoking sorrow and at the same time hope. Sorrow, arising from a place and time from which I feel exiled; hope, because the place evoked, and towards which I am drawn, is one where in a time gone by the most intense of desires has been satisfied and where perhaps, in a time to come, such satisfaction may be known again.

That place, that lost time, is indicated by a name: 'beauty', and it is the memory of the experience of beauty which arouses nostalgia. To remember is in fact to replace in the heart (in Italian 'ri-cordare') what had at one time filled it. Once, the heart had called 'beauty' the splendour of a harmony reached without human intent, the spontaneous gift of meaning coming with the unexpected, luminous revelation of a part of the cosmos—at that moment no longer a part but the whole. That was the revelation beheld by Plato, and he defined forever 'beauty' as the manifestation of eternal being in a fragment of the world and of time.

The exile of beauty is though an inevitable condition, because beauty reveals itself in a place and time to which it does not belong, the place and time of an apparition and of a corresponding state of the soul, which I now remember and for which I feel nostalgia. Beauty is the way in which the eternal manifests itself in time, and time and the eternal coincide in kairos, the moment, again as Plato recalled. Thus, beauty and transience reveal themselves together and at the same instant, an instant which cannot but cause me to feel sorrow at exile and hope for return.

Beauty reveals itself, said Plotinus, to those with a lover's heart. It arouses the ardour of Eros, but only in those who yield themselves to Eros. Eros is the yearning for the eternal in the soul, taking form in the vision of beauty. Eros is replaced by a kindred daimon, Pothos, 'nostalgia', when all that remains of the vision of beauty is memory. The ancients therefore entrusted to Mnemosyne, memory, the mother of the Muses, those arts which allow man to awaken and at the same time to placate the nostalgia for beauty, by remembering the numerous forms in which beauty has revealed itself to the soul. Mnemosyne leads us away from chronological time—the time of Cronos who devours his children, annihilating every event of being—into a timeless time, a place that is nowhere, in the imaginal world where time and eternity interweave in images which are not temporal and do not belong to the eternal.

We can therefore understand the imagination of an artist as being like the power of Mnemosyne in one of the forms in which she is manifest in time—a form the ancients called 'Muse'. The artist is then the man of memory and he evokes for us those aspects of the imaginal world vouchsafed to him. He can do this because he has known, perhaps more intensely than others, that beauty and transience are intimately linked, and that beauty appears not but in things that pass, and their passing is perceived as even more inexorable and heart-rending when beauty has been made manifest in them. Thus the artist must hold indissolubly united in his heart the incandescent splendour of beauty, with the fullness of sense welling from it, and the dark impending presence of death, when every sense fades. This is the terrible agon, the agony of the artist who stakes at the same time the possibility that there be both his art and his personal existence, his twofold and convergent task of individuation.

What has remained—of this picture testifying to the greatness evoked by so many artists—in the linguistic elucubrations rife in our time? It does not even seem a time of exile, as the lost land of beauty seems to have been completely forgotten. Wherein lies the error which has meant condemnation to aimless wandering, to the futility of a devouring time abandoning the past unmourned, where there is no redemption by greatness, memory, beauty?

Perhaps it is not really beauty which has been repressed, and not memory. Perhaps what has been removed is the premise for both: not the eternal, but the transient, not the general, but the particular. It is death which has been repressed, and the infinite compassion which death engenders, if we have a lover's heart. Art, though, originated from death, was born of mourning, in the memory of what was loved and is no longer: the presence, radiant with beauty, that had aroused love.

When subjectivity arrogantly takes centre stage, when knowledge of reality is reduced to a function of the subject and no longer appears as a spontaneous opening of the world comprising subject and object in transcendent intimacy, then the incandescent knowledge which springs forth from this all-embracing unfolding dies down, and the flame of love at its heart is extinguished. The only reality deemed worthy of the name, the subject, remains, with its narcissistic hybris, swelling proportionately to the abyss that separates the subject from both the transience and loveliness of the world. No longer are there things which he can evoke with love and sorrow, tenderness and wonder: all that exists is his language, to be exhibited in its infinite variations, and his talking of nothing.

Death is removed from the subject, because apart from him, nothing irreplaceable is left, nothing to be lost and mourned. This is the domain of complete nihilism.

If therefore the art critic concentrates on language and judges the value of a work in terms of the apparent novelty of its idiom instead of its meaning, and if artists too lend themselves compliantly to such criticism, they also distinguishing language from what calls it into being, or the need for an image to become present, then the image is lost. And what is improperly still called art lacks its end and meaning: access to the imaginal world. The imaginal world, or the world which manifests in beauty, is lost, and with it transcendence and meaning. There is no more art, even less is there criticism of art, because there is no longer any way of distinguishing art from what is not art. There is only the will to exercise power of the autonomous subject, deaf to the voice of poetry, for poetry does not come from the subject but emanates from the soul of the world, as Boccaccio said.

When the image is there, when it is not a mere hieroglyphic but a living presence of the imaginal world, it invites silence and contemplation. We can speak of it, but as we would of a living being, or an event, and since every image imagines and causes imagining, that is, it carries us with it into the imaginal world, we can talk of it as of an apparition which moves us and arouses memories and reflections. The artist, too, then withdraws into the background, as do history and linguistic and formal analyses. The image remains, with its evocative power, and the love it arouses in us at the beauty to which it bears witness: a beauty which it recalls for us, by which it awakens us and draws us forth.

Beauty evoked by art is manifested in different materials and forms according to the imagination recalling it. Here I shall refer only to painting. For the painter, the image reveals itself as a body of light, while the formless, from which it emerges and differentiates itself, is darkness for him. So it seems that the painter is destined to labour in the darkness, in that twilight which is proper to painting—as Titian said—or in the imaginal place where light and shadow mesh and struggle, where shadow menaces the light which illuminates it. In this tension, which traverses and travails the soul of the painter, form is freed from the formless which constantly assails it. And yet painting has progressively lost the mystery of this archetypal struggle, when its calling is to bear witness to that struggle. That mystery has been slipping away for more than a century, since imaginal light began to be reduced to natural light, and even more, since the Impressionists subjected the light of painting to the positivism of their analyses. Thus did they favour the linguistic reduction of images which was to become widespread after them: a reduction of the image to a sign that robbed colour and representation of light and imaginal quality, so condemning painting to death. There have however been other painters, aware of the drama being played out, who have obdurately resisted such obscuration and loss of light. They have been misunderstood even when their worth has been acknowledged, for the fundamental meaning of their work and the defence they were constructing with it went unrecognised.

What is essential for us in the works of those masters is the need to return to that inner state whereby it is possible to go to painting as to an initiatory path along which light reveals itself. Only in this light found anew can painting fulfil its original meaning and become regenerated, recalling once more for us the transient presences of this world, and the beauty of their revelation, with its heart-rending nostalgia.

One of those masters, Giorgio Morandi, was well aware of this when in 1925, at the age of thirty five, he painted one of his rare self-portraits, today in the Fondazione Magnani Rocca.

Giorgio Morandi, Self-portrait, 1925

Here the painter is seated with simple dignity in front of an invisible easel. He is dressed like any worker, in a waistcoat, with a collarless shirt, his hands holding brushes and pallet, the tools of his trade. In this self-portrait Morandi, immersed in light, himself a 'body of light', like the objects he was representing, established an indissoluble continuity between the painter and his objects, a continuity provided by the substance they share: light. His unwavering gaze, turned both inwards and outwards, transformed those objects into light, as the picture shows. It is almost as if he had wished to give visible form to a traditional prescription, expressed by Dante in a page of his *Convivio*: 'He who paints a figure, if he cannot become it, cannot render it' (*Convivio* IV, Canzone, vv. 52-53). The painter, likening himself to imaginal light, thus becomes its custodian. His painting was keeper of the light, which transformed him and temporal things into presences of the imaginal world . Light here is not natural and not even metaphysical, because it is not separated from the singularity of things. Instead it needs their spatial determination if it is to manifest, for it requires the particular, irreplaceable emotional link which recognises and animates them.

Morandi, therefore, had positioned the painter as a guardian of images and their ontological dignity, but as such he was also guardian of the intimate fragility from which they originate and are made. This secret dignity showed itself to him in the cloister-like space of his studio and in his small pictures. It was revealed only with an opening up to the impermanence of things and their imminent dissolution, and thus entrusted to ordinary objects and places without importance, encountered in every day life, things already being inevitably devoured by time. The dignity is absolute and essential just because there is no trace of glory to sustain it in these objects. We can recognize it, for example, in a still-life painted in 1942.

Giorgio Morandi, Still Life, 1942

If we contemplate that array of silent objects, each humbly affirming its own presence, fragile but unique and irreplaceable. The dignity lies in the absolute absence of any excess, in occupying a 'position' which is necessary for that radiation of light, in accord with the whole. In each of his works, Morandi invites us to a meditation not only on the things of the world, but also on the figures of the soul. Neither is destined to prevail, although emphasis shifts from one to the other, as they are each a different degree of light, a passage, a link which could not be dissolved without dissolving the whole. Each is an opportunity for light, a determination of it, an illumination of detail, calmly and steadily radiating from the particular to the whole.

The material with which Morandi painted was devoid of splendour, like the objects he represented, and appears dusty and impure, withholding light and slowly yielding it. Light emanates from the lumps of paint on the canvas as from the inner nature of things. It is a light absorbed in matter and which becomes matter, while matter, given substance by the light, is transubstantiated, becoming itself a body of light, the visible symbol of the invisible weft giving form to a cosmos.

That same year, 1925, Edouard Vuillard painted his friend Pierre Bonnard, another solitary master.

Edouard Vuillard, Bonnard in front of one of his canvases, 1925

He had surprised Bonnard observing a canvas he was painting, stretched on the wall of a room with none of the characteristics of a studio, a simple, middle-class sitting room. This was a normal situation for Bonnard, who favoured settings which were part of his daily existence. He tacked his canvases to a wall and only stretched them for mounting at the end, when he was able to define the confines and space of the image he had painted. He could not do so before, because the image he was seeking was taking form not in accordance with any plan but gradually, as it was being painted, and was therefore helped by the absence of any pre-defined limit. Thus uncertainty about the emerging image remained throughout, with the anxiety accompanying its striving for form.

This anxiety was captured by Vuillard just as Bonnard was stepping back to examine his work, slipping from one state of attention to another, his body poised in precarious equilibrium. Vuillard had captured the moment when the painter became his own critic, distanced yet involved, showing empathy with the emerging image, thereby defining an attitude appropriate for the simple contemplation of an image.

Bonnard is looking, thinking, tentatively exploring with his imagination to find the point of balance where form in its completion is revealed. He questions both the image and himself. Perhaps the image will finally radiate light, the image as the splendour of form, the successful manifestation of the invisible, whose call Bonnard has been following as he has been painting. Or perhaps the image has not yet fulfilled its destiny, is not yet a living, autonomous being, has not yet emerged, and the matter which has gone into its making has not yet been transmuted into soul. 'It is not a question of painting life, but of making the painting live', he said (Terrase 1984, p.202). Thus, he was wondering what was to be done, where a touch was needed, where the opacity of the matter was still resisting light in its striving to burst forth from within and confer life, the light he can see but not quite find. 'It is only colour, not yet light…' (Terrasse 1984, p.178)

Sometimes, when an old man, Bonnard would look in the same way at a painting of his hanging in a museum, and would be disturbed, realizing that zones of colour had escaped his control and now seemed to him to be without light, to cause a dull alteration of the image. The old artist, his pocket full of tubes of pigment, would hide from the custodians to continue his work at night, until light was visible everywhere in the picture.

Similarly, in 1946, he returned to a self-portrait painted three years previously and already published in a book by André Lhote.

Pierre Bonnard, Self-portrait, 1946

Again he had captured himself before the mirror of a dressing table, not in his studio but amongst the things and gestures of daily life, the perennial subjects of his painting. Or perhaps it would be better to say that his work, once he was beyond the age of thirty five, had become more and more a vision of time, of its silently shifting colours, as we could define memory when entrusted to the images of painting.

Then he was seventy six years old and living in retirement at Le Cannet. Two years previously his friend Vuillard had died, and afterwards Marthe, his life long companion. The Bonnard in the mirror was naked, more helpless than ever. He died a year after having returned to the painting, which remained beside him to the end. Unclothed, his bare flesh exposed, he showed as never before a timid vulnerability in the display of his spare, sunken body, his very essence, the source of his yearning for beauty.

It was wrongly thought afterwards that Bonnard had been inspired by the bodies of the survivors of Auschwitz or Bergen-Belsen, but as we have seen, this painting dates from 1943. This error shows how profoundly though discreetly Bonnard had come to evoke sorrow, bewilderment, the nearness of death, his own and that of everything he loved, and how compassionate his gaze had become.

We can suppose that he had arrived at this achievement because he had not repressed the feeling of melancholy at the transience allied inevitably with every moment of happiness, or rather because he had recognized in this feeling of transience the diffuse welcoming light illuminating a memorable image of the fleeting moment, a revelation of Kairos, the time of his painting. We read, in a notebook form 1939, 'The point lies in the meeting of nature and the inner feeling of beauty', and from a page written a few days later: 'In that moment in which we say we are happy, we are so no longer'(Terrase 1984, p.198). At the origin of his paintings was that meeting and that joyful moment, together with sorrow at their inevitable loss.

Why such anxiety, in a painter? It was a valuable anxiety, already considered by Picasso to be the real lesson learned from Cézanne. 'What is really interesting', he said, 'is Cézanne's anxiety' (Berger 1996, p.22). The roots of that anxiety stretched far, even if Cézanne more than others had brought it into focus, keeping it at the critical centre of his work. It had in fact arisen when the canons of the Academy had proved no longer able to guide the formative process of images. Such canons had for a long time provided the sole way of seeing images, and they had in the end served only to tame them into well-tried forms, copying the great examples of the sixteenth and seventeenth centuries. The move to abandon those canons had begun precisely because they suffocated and constrained images, preventing them from manifesting as other than complaisant allusions to a past, albeit a noble one.

The Academy no longer provided the means to give form to images, to lead them to a more complete expression and manifestation of their mysterious life. Rather, images were subjected to conventions and thus exorcised, robbed of their power to emerge for themselves. Reducing images to their mere appearance in the end disguised a void: the fact that they were really absent, out of reach. Devotion to images had been lost, conquered by fear at their daimon-like independence. Art had been reduced to a complex and masterly performance of slight of hand, with the purpose of conferring prestige upon the artist, exalting his skill, invention and humanistic culture, and upon the gentlemen displaying art in their dwellings. Beauty finally seemed available, defined by a canon of harmony, images reduced to 'beautiful things'. And if sometimes we glimpse true beauty in one of those works, if a daimon bursts through just the same, it is not in obedience to those canons but despite them, because of that violence the invisible sometimes displays in order to find a way of taking visible form.

Kantian enlightenment had abetted the Academy , dispatching art to a zone of 'disinterest'—art for art's sake—which was possible only if critical clarification had banished every manifestation of a daimon to the shadows. Thus, throughout the nineteenth century, from Goya to Cézanne, those artists who were dedicated to the art of evoking images rather than to art for art's sake found that that they had to face the daimon returning from exile, stirring an obscure inner impulse and engendering relentless anxiety. These artists had thus rediscovered something which had been lost, the possibility of being involved in what their art could evoke, an involvement carried to the point where they staked their very lives. Their passion tolled the death knell of a whole aesthetic vision, one expressed by the dispassionate Academy.

It was the young Picasso who at the age of twenty five sanctioned this transformation when he painted *Les Demoiselles d'Avignon* and evoked the magic power of tribal masks whose power touched the painted images, so that they were no longer 'representations' but explicit 'presentations' of the daimons of the soul, forms of the pathos which swirl obscurely in its depths. It was 1907, the year in which Jung published his essay on the dementia praecox, the study in which he started to recognize those daimons as at the origin of the dissociation of the anima in independent fragments, in distinct and conflicting personifications of pathos.

The pathos of the image had become the inner referent and guide in the process of taking form. A dionisiac ethos had entered the care of the soul, bringing together artists and the pioneers of psychology, in particular Jung, occupied with his 'dialogue with the unconscious'. It was for the individual to recognize, in the pandemonium of images, those whose pathos governed his soul, and to care for them, ensuring for them an appropriate manifestation in the world.

An enduring sign of this ethical tension—the inner agon between acceptance of and fleeing from the daimonic image—was anxiety, and the necessary attack on the reification of beauty, a constant of western culture. The possible gain was great: the awakening of a memory which seemed lost, the return to the original sense of beauty, no longer confined to academic canons and conventional taste, but found where it was always waiting, in every manifestation of being, however terrible.

All this is evident in the paintings of Zoran Music, the oldest of the living masters. Music had been deported to Dachau at the age of thirty five, and in the weeks before liberation, when supervision had slackened, he was able to sketch his dying companions as they drew their last breaths, and their corpses, piled into heaps. Many years later he was to recount how as he looked at those tortured bodies, he was attracted by their incomprehensible beauty. 'How much tragic elegance in those fragile limbs. Such precise detail. Those hands, the thin fingers, the feet. The mouths gaping in their last attempt to gasp some air. The white, almost bluish skin stretched over the bones. How much zeal to avoid betraying those subtle forms, to render them precious as I saw them, reduced to the essential. I was as if gripped by a fever, with the irresistible need to draw so that this grandiose and tragic beauty would not escape me' (Peppiett 2000b, p.34).

Twenty five years were to pass before, in 1970, Music could return to those images. For five years he evoked their presence in his painting until he could say that those corpses had become riches for him, the inner place where he could go for inspiration when the force of imagination waned.

Zoran Music, We are not the Last, 1975

Once he wrote: 'I hope that this vision of death will remain forever in my unconscious.' He had a dream in which he was surrounded by his companions, who suddenly began to disperse, while he woke up abruptly, terrified at having lost what he treasured.

Aged seventy eight, aware that the light of painting might die out in him, Music once again turned to his dead, allowing the wound to reopen. Once more he depicted the infernal beauty of those corpses. It was 1987. This return led to a new season, the last of his life and art. The following year he began to paint several self-portraits where his face, as not in the past, began to resemble those of the dead of Dachau. There is the same matter, the same light. The hues of life and death, which until then had been kept distinct, almost as if signifying the different light coming from two different kingdoms, are now merged one with the other, so that life and death can no longer be discerned with certainty, perhaps because his life was by then awakening to death. The light was dim, spectral, from the underworld, and looking at it, it is impossible to know whether it emerges from the dark or is about to be forever absorbed into it. This is a light which comes from old age—that middle ground between life and death—and which illuminates it.

A destiny is fulfilled in these paintings. Reified beauty, available in an ideal form, disappears. It no longer even seems appreciable and gives way to an unexpected daimonic beauty which comes from the world and penetrates the soul, destroying any reassuring vision. This is a beauty which springs only from that spontaneous revelation, blazing forth as and where it will.

The anxiety accompanying the work of these artists is born of an inner obligation, a daimon of the soul: the need to keep the fragments in which time is manifest securely connected to the eternal, which confers form and meaning upon them. This in an age which instead constructs its present on the rubble of memory. Artists point the way for us, because they struggle with and vanquish the formless, to win that middle ground which is the basis for our feeling of a living, animated reality: image, beauty, symbol, or the conjunction of the temporal and the eternal, of the personal and the archetypal. This is why they know that life itself is at stake.

Art is an interpretation. It is born of the gaze which sees the forms of time emerge from their archetypal weft, and holds them interwoven. When we approach art, however we do so, the arguments we put forward must be the same as those we use for any other interpretation of an archetypal reality. Firstly, we must not dissolve it, reducing it to what is merely natural, or particular and historical, thus irreparably tearing the fabric of art and bringing about a splitting in the soul. Art is in fact governed by Mnemosyne, because it is the memory of the archetypal background, and its images are the roots we seek to keep ourselves safe, reaching deep into the soul. Any interpretation cleaving those roots would irrevocably damage art, our care of it, and its care of our soul. Jung, in his essay in the archetype of the puer, recalled that '….each new degree of differentiation of consciousness must contend with the task of finding a new 'interpretation', suitable to the new degree reached, and therefore able to link up past life, still living in us, with present life, which threatens to break away from it. If this does not happen, consciousness is uprooted, disorientated…' Art is one of the forms in which this new and necessary interpretation is brought about, it is a way of 'dreaming of' the myth giving it a modern form, but, as Jung warned, '… whatever explanation or interpretation does to it [myth], we do to our own souls as well, with corresponding results for our own well-being' (Jung 1949a, par. 271). This holds good for the artist's interpretation, but also for that of any one approaching a work of art. It is permitted to no one therefore to approach images without risk to the soul coming from the interpretation we provide of those images, or from the way in which we take them into our life, an art in its turn. Anxiety is necessary for us as well, just as it is born of the awareness of that danger, but also of the possible gain. It is a legacy we carry with us from the century which has just run its course—the example of Cézanne, the heritage of Jung.

APPENDIX II

Memory of the Invisible

A comparison of Northern and Southern Images

Diane Finiello Zervas and Francesco Donfrancesco

When Jung published *On the Nature of the Psyche* near the end of his life (Jung1954b), he reconfirmed the non-scientific nature of his psychology, emphasising its subjective and narrative character. For those of us who accept and wish to advance this aspect of our Jungian heritage, it is crucial to assume a critical-hermeneutic attitude; moreover, we must attempt to understand Jung's ideas within their proper historical and cultural context. Indeed, his thought does not attempt to 'explain' the life of the psyche, but rather to 'interpret' it. Interpretation implies 'pre-comprehension', particularly a framework of cultural reference, which in Jung's case had its origins in Goethe and the Pietistic, Protestant aspects of the Northern Romantic movement.

Under such circumstances, those of us with a Mediterranean background are, by contrast, often and forcibly confronted by the 'Germanic' aspects of Jung's culture and psyche. His inability to reach Rome represents the most evident symptom of a dramatic tension between North and South. Indeed, it was Hillman, in his 1973 lecture 'Plotino, Ficino and Vico as Precursors of Archetypal Psychology', delivered in Rome, who emphasised that the numinous effect 'Italy' had on Jung, and his inability to reach the Eternal City, were aspects of his 'Italian' complex. Drawing on López-Pedraza's concept of a geographical and historical complex, Hillman noted that Italy is not only the 'underside, the compensatory land of the "unconscious"' for Northern, Protestant peoples, but also the 'specific geographical and historical psychic complexity that is implied in the image "Italy", and which Jung sensed in the meanings and emotions that were unleashed by the image "Rome"'. Hillman suggested that an exploration of 'Italian' thought, culture, and images would help complete that lacuna in Jung's own perspective, and thus Jungian psychology, in regard to 'Italy', thereby helping to extend the field of Jung's psychology (Hillman 1973, p.160).

Following this lead, we intend to explore, develop, and contrast the Northern and Southern approaches to the image, suggesting a dialogue between the two different forms of artistic and psychological sensibilities, especially by means of images taken from paintings. In Jung's case, the emphasis is always placed on the symbolic value of the image. The visible—the perceptible—is merely the portal that leads to the true reality beyond the perceptible world, the realm of the archetypal images, manifestations of the invisible and unknowable archetypes. Mistrusting the aesthetic experience of the image, Jung placed the emphasis on its meaning –iconology—that could help to reveal its unpredictable and mysterious nature. His approach favours an art that is numinous and visionary, attributes that 18th-century aestheticians associated with 'the Sublime'.

By contrast, the Mediterranean tradition, based on Orthodoxy and Catholicism, is basically iconophilic. The image is treated not as a symbolic representation or an allusion to an ulterior reality, but rather as a 'presentation', as a 'presence' that reveals itself; and the *aisthesis*—sensate knowledge—as its form of knowing. Here the emphasis is placed on the harmonious experience of the 'Beautiful', rather than the awesome experience of the 'Sublime'.

Just as many of Jung's ideas about analytical psychology were nurtured in the womb of Romantic and neo-Romantic philosophy, so many of his theories about artists, the creative process, and the work of art were indebted to concepts of these earlier movements. They formed part of his educational background, and he had studied German Romantic philosophers, poets and aestheticians while researching *Psychology of the Unconscious* (1916b) and *Psychological Types* (1921). Indeed, in his spoken introduction to 'Psychology and Literature', composed sometime after 1930, he acknowledges his debt to Bachofen, Carus, Schopenhauer and von Hartmann (Jung 1966,7).

In *Psychological Types*, Jung associated two irrational typologies with the artistic personality, namely introverted sensation and intuition, but his Idealistic leanings, his own typology, and the images that had appeared during his confrontation with the unconscious served to focus his attention on the introverted intuitive artist. Attracted to the inner object, or, if stimulated by external objects, concerned with 'what the external object has released within him', the introverted intuitive artist moves 'from image to image, chasing after every possibility in the teeming womb of the unconscious', thereby apprehending 'images arising from the *a priori* inherited foundations of the unconscious'—the archetypes (Jung 1921, pars. 656, 658, 659).

Jung continued to develop his ideas on art over the next decade, turning his attention to the process of artistic creation and the work of art. Rejecting Freud's personal and reductive view of art, Jung felt that a 'true work of art' escapes personal limitations and soars beyond its creator's personal concerns, having been produced by an autonomous creative complex that overwhelms him with a 'flood of thoughts and images which he never intended to create', but which is nevertheless 'his own self speaking', his 'own inner nature' revealing itself. Such a work of art is symbolic, revealing an archetypal image from the collective unconscious, or, in the terms of our dialogue, making visible the invisible. Furthermore, Jung stressed that by giving this image shape, 'the artist translates it into the language of the present, and so makes it possible for us to find our way back to the deepest springs of life. Therein lies the social significance of art: it is constantly at work educating the spirit of the age, conjuring up the forms in which the age is most lacking' (Jung 1966,6, pars. 107, 109, 130).

The art created by the great German Romantic artist, Casper David Friedrich (1774-1840) exemplifies many of these Jungian concepts. Working in Dresden, Friedrich was familiar with many of the city's leading philosophers and writers, who perceived his art as the visual embodiment of their ideals. Strongly influenced by the transcendentalism that the Romantics derived from Kant, Friedrich was also, for a time, supported by Goethe, and he was a close friend and informal teacher of the artist and critic Carl Gustav Carus (1789-1869), whose book *Psyche* (1846) Jung so admired. He never left Germany; thus, like Jung, he never visited Rome.

Reacting against the Enlightenment, the philosophical and artistic ideals of German Romanticism placed prime importance on the individual, imagination, and feeling. Fundamental to this view is the notion of the Divine in nature, and nature as an inner voice or impulse, which man can only know by expressing what he finds within him. By reconnecting with his emotional response to nature, the Romantic artist makes his inner vision manifest in a work of art, as evident in Friedrich's beautiful landscape, *Large Enclosure* (1832), where the earth and water repeat and reflect the almost divinely lit shapes in the heavens. (And the extent to which Jung was indebted to such Romantic visions is immediately evident in one of his rare paintings of 1904, *Lake Constance*).

Caspar David Friedrich, Large Enclosure, ca. 1832

Carl Gustav Jung, Lake Constance, 1904

Especially important was F.W. Schelling's 'nature philosophy', which emphasised that it was man's awareness both of himself and of the world around him that brought the unconscious life in nature to conscious expression. Schelling believed that the plastic arts of painting and sculpture provided an active bond (in Jung's terms a mediating function) between the soul and nature, an infusion of the material with the spiritual. The artist must grasp the essential, instinctive spirit of nature, 'working at the core of things and speak[ing] through signs and shapes as by symbols only', realising ideas that were previously obscure and unintelligible autonomously, through his unique genius (Vaughan 1980, p.66). In this way, he 'Romanticises the World', fashioning each object as if it were the bearer of some higher significance, the culmination of a quest, an altar to the hidden God. Thus, each object becomes a symbol within a symbolic whole.

Friedrich strongly believed that the artist 'must learn by experiencing, become the thing in order to get to know the soul and even the underlying form of nature'. His surviving sketchbooks attest to his repeated excursions into the wild, where he made detailed drawings of natural motifs, as, for example a *Study of Fir Trees*, dated 28 April 1807.

At the upper right, he has sketched a tree in its entirety, abstracting it from its natural surroundings. Below, he begins to reduce the motif further, concentrating on its outlines. Such sketches formed the raw material for his paintings. By capturing each object's uniqueness in a recorded moment of time, Friedrich's sketchbooks embody his lived experience; they form the *prima materia* of *Erlebniskunst*: art that comes from, and is an expression of the artist's inner response to experience.

But the creative process itself occurred within Friedrich's studio, as is evident in the *Portrait of Friedrich* made by fellow artist Georg Friedrich Kersting in 1819 . Its monk-like simplicity, uncluttered by props or sketches, with the window semi-shuttered to concentrate the light and obscure any outside view, enabled him to bring forth the invisible. Entreating his fellow artists to 'close your bodily eye so that you may see your painting first with the spiritual eye, then bring to the light of day that which you have seen in the darkness so that it may react upon others from the outside inwards' Friedrich affirmed that 'a feeling, darkly intuiting, and rarely fully clear to the artist himself, always underlies his pictures'. And Carus described how, before beginning a picture, Friedrich would wait until the image 'stood lifelike in his mind's eye', and then would quickly begin to work, sketching it first on the bare canvas in chalk and pencil, and then in pen and ink, followed immediately by the underpainting (Vaughan 1980, p.68). Only then would he turn to his nature-sketches, employing them for particular details, often reusing them in different works.

The *Winter Landscape with a Church,* finished in 1811 is an early example of Friedrich's Romantic ideals.

Caspar David Friedrich, Winter Landscape with a Church, 1811

In the midst of a desolate winter landscape, we find a small *Rückenfigur,* a halted traveller. He rests against a jutting boulder, praying to a wooden Crucifix in a pine grove, a natural apse, composed of firs similar to those sketched in 1807. To his left stand further groves, and other boulders, their forms suggestive of gravestones. The cast-off crutches suggest the traveller's precarious state, and signpost his path of arrival, stretching diagonally up from the lower right corner. Critics have noted that the central fir grove would have obscured his view of the church that rises in ethereal fashion from the thick mist in the distance, its multiple spires echoing the firs' natural forms.

The painting intimates man's earthly search for the Divine, whose forms are present in the material, perennial firs and ancient rocks, suggestive of nature's everlasting life, and suggested by the fog-veiled cathedral, his ultimate spiritual destination, an Idea almost visible. The winter season mirrors the traveller's state, close to the end of his mortal journey. He and the artist have become one, registering that what we, the viewers, see, is not a natural landscape, but Friedrich's *Erlebnis,* his temporal experience of nature re-imagined, a memory of the invisible made visible.

The Wanderer above a Sea of Mist painted about 1818, at the height of the German Romantic movement, is a multi-layered, symbolic and truly visionary work of art.

Caspar David Friedrich, Wanderer above a Sea of Mist ca. 1818

In Friedrich's earlier works, the *Rückenfigur* was placed within the landscape, but here he is monumentalised. Placed almost exactly in the centre of the painting, he stands on the summit of the rocky foreground promontory with his back to us, partially obscuring the seemingly infinite view beyond. By these means, Friedrich forces us to view the painting as if we were the halted traveller. Moreover, all the landscape elements, from the foreground irregular rocky triangle through the isolated and dipping intermediate tree-crowned ridges to the more distant ranges and mountain peaks, are fragments that converge on him. Without him, the composition falls to pieces in the foggy mist, which in any case serves to cancel distance and perspective.

Here Friedrich is fully engaged in the aesthetics of the Sublime. The new iconography of mountains and evocative rock formations emphasise the awesome, the wilfully obscure, the moment in which the painting attempts to reveal the infinite; in this case the mystical infinity of nature in the halted traveller's heart, upon which the two central diagonals of the distant ranges converge. As such Friedrich's painting is the objectification, a re-membering of a multi-layered subjective experience.

In Carus's letters on landscape painting, he states that fog was God's assistant at creation (Carus 1972). In the *Wanderer above the Sea of Mist,* it is also a symbol of the creative power of the artist, who does not imitate nature's products, but rather nature's unending creative process. Yet Friedrich makes us aware that we, too, must participate directly in what we see. Indeed, there are three creative imaginations involved in viewing this work: the artist's, the halted traveller's, and our own. Thus Friedrich's *Rückenfigur* is also an image of the multiplicity of the invisible Self.

Friedrich created a very different mood in *The Sea of Ice* executed about 1824.

Caspar David Friedrich, The Sea of Ice, ca. 1823/24

The painting is related to the destroyed *Shipwreck on the Coast of Greenland* that was commissioned by the future Zarina of Russia, Alexandra Feodorova, after a visit by her husband, Grand-Duke Nicholas, to Friedrich's studio in Dresden in December 1820. She had requested Friedrich to paint a subject representing Nordic nature in all its 'fearsome beauty,' to serve as a pendant to another lost work extolling the generous beauty of nature in the Southern climes: in other words, the pair were to express the theme of the Sublime and the Beautiful in terms of the North and South.

Like *The Wanderer above a Sea of Mist*, *The Sea of Ice* is deeply symbolic, containing multiple levels of meaning. Although individual pictorial elements refer to precise studies made of the break-up of ice on the Elbe by Friedrich during the winter of 1820-21, they also recall a tragic event from his childhood nearly forty years earlier, when one of his elder brothers drowned while attempting to rescue Friedrich during an ice-skating outing on the Baltic. Here, however, there is no human presence, just a fragmented product of human craft, the crushed prow and mast of a sailing ship trapped by the Sublimely destructive artic ice. A metaphor of the Romantics' crushed political hopes under Metternich, the painting has also been called a *navigatio vitae* that represents man's mortal journey, whose course leads inevitably to death, but now without the redeeming Crucifix and cathedral of the earlier *Winter Landscape with Church*. And it is also an image of psyche frozen in the sharp shards of an icy wasteland, a votive offering and witness to man's frail struggle to transcend the empty, hostile wastes of extreme experience.

Significantly, in Friedrich's own time *The Sea of Ice* was rejected by the general public. The work of a true visionary artist who 'bodies forth the shape of things unseen' the painting also depicts an era about to be crushed by its opposite, the frigid, soulless wasteland of materialist culture, so despised by Jung, which would only begin to thaw again during his youth.

The painters we are going to look at now were for the most part born in Tuscany during the last fifteen years of Friedrich's life. They began to associate with one another in Florence in the second half of the 1850s, meeting at the Caffè Michelangelo, where their passionate discussions of art became interlaced with debates over the 'rebirth of Italy' and the struggle for the country's unification, in which they played an active part.

Until just a few years earlier, the somewhat sheepish expression of nationalistic feelings had been confined to nostalgia for days of glory in the remote past, and in their historical pictures artists had compensated for a humiliating present with the rhetoric of a greatness of which, in reality, only traces remained. With the proclamation of the Kingdom of Italy in 1861, and of Florence as its capital in 1865, their exile came to an end, their common home was rediscovered and, even though a residual fragmentation of the country remained, the process of integration had reached an irreversible stage. Now the dignity of a daily life at last set free and able to proceed in peace called out for representation: city streets, cloisters, the interiors of houses and family affections, work in the fields, military life. A time that had seemed lost forever emerged again, the time of a harmony regained; and those images, almost always painted on a small scale, quietly acknowledged its presence.

And it was in that very year of 1861 that these artists started to paint *en plein air*—as we are shown in a small picture by Giovanni Fattori, *Silvestro Lega Painting on the Rocks*—before returning to the studio to finish the work. Immersed in the radiance of nature to the point where they felt as if they were part of a Pandean continuum, they studied the expressive 'effects' of natural light at length, and in their painting sought those subtle nuances of light and shade that would allow the space of the picture to take on a life of its own, and find order and harmony through rhythm and measure.

Raffaello Sernesi, who was twenty-three at the time, spent the summer of that year with the twenty-eight-year-old Odoardo Borrani on the highest of the mountains that stand between Florence and the sea, where he painted *Mountain Pasture*.

Raffaello Sernesi, Mountain Pasture, 1861

It is not easy to describe the absolute and solemn simplicity of this image, the crystalline brilliance that gives it form. An absorbed silence can be heard, the wonder of an apparition that has nothing unexpected about it: a calm ecstasy. The slow passage of the herdswoman and the cows, the sparse trees and the frayed white clouds all follow a harmonious rhythm, which infects anyone who looks at the picture; and who is thus able to experience that crucial moment in which the eternal succeeds in shining through an image of time, a revelation in the apparition, that sudden vision of the cosmos in just one facet of existence that has been called 'beauty' ever since the time of Plato. Caught up in the contemplation, we discover its form: the light, the space, the time in which it occurs.

It is an Apollonian contemplation into which we are drawn, as intimate as a statue of Apollo attributed to Praxiteles which can be seen in the Vatican Museums. The smiling god is aiming an arrow at a lizard, motionless on the trunk of a tree: at a soul in search of light, which has halted in ecstatic abandon, transfixed by a ray of sunlight. The yearning of the soul for light and the gratuitous gift to it of the divine light is the mystery celebrated, the event, at once human and divine, of that mutual contemplation in which lies the essence of every mysticism of light. And we know from his letters and declarations that the young Sernesi was conscious of this.

As observers of the painting, we are like that humble lizard of Mediterranean walls, feeling ourselves to be as small as the woman herding the cows, and sharing with her in the wonder that pervades everything. 'Know thyself' was written on the pediment of the temple of Apollo at Delphi: recognize yourself as a tiny human being before the awesome calm of the gods. This is the beginning of the illumination that Apollo gives. The vision is granted to an ordinary human being, who feels him or herself to be just like everyone else, and not to a monk, to a solitary thinker, to a visionary hero, as in Friedrich.

Three years later, during the summer of 1864, Odoardo Borrani painted *Diego's Garden at Castiglioncello*.

Odoardo Borrani, Diego's Garden at Castiglioncello, 1864

This picture reveals the maturity now attained by Borrani's vision, in the complete osmosis between ideal form and analysis of observed reality, in the awareness of the spontaneous classicism hidden in the forms of nature and, in particular, in the discovery of the intimate cohesion between art and nature, between the work of man and natural growth, so characteristic of the Tuscan landscape, modelled down the centuries by the constant and patient labour of peasants.

All this is recomposed, and revealed to the gaze, in an instant, when the peasant working in his vegetable garden stops, lifts his head as if in response to a silent and invisible call, and remains motionless, overcome with wonder at an accustomed beauty. The peasant's, Borrani's and our own gaze coincide, seeing in an indeterminable moment and from an indeterminable point in space, drawn into the centre of a harmony that embraces everything: both the animate and the inanimate. Apollo's gaze is turned on this fragment of the world, it has made the visible transparent: the invisible revealed is here, here its eternal presence is unveiled. The gods are not other or elsewhere: now we know like Thales that 'all things are full of gods'.

Sernesi and Borrani had absorbed the lesson of Augusto Conti, a Florentine philosopher who in those years invited his students to reconcile heart and mind, realism and idealism. Bringing about this reconciliation in painting entailed being faithful to an analytical observation of the world, like the one suggested by the dominant positivistic culture. But it was precisely through this careful observation of the aspects of the world that it became possible to uncover in them the inner geometries, the measure and proportions that had animated the ideal, Neoplatonic vision of the great Tuscan masters of the 15th century, to whom these painters never ceased to look. Thus time and eternity, present and past, found the intuitive point and the form in which to remain united. Years later Cézanne was to see things in a similar way, setting out 'to do Poussin again, from Nature': going back to tradition, rediscovered however in the contemplation of his own land, of its light, revealed in nature as implicit, harmonious, eternal measure, as its archetypal structure—"*son classicisme*", as Cézanne called it. And the inner form that generated this classicism, and continues still and forever to generate it, is what resurfaces of necessity in every true rebirth, or *risorgimento*, as it was referred to in the Italy of our painters' time: the solid, lasting foundation of a culture, wherein lies the energy capable of being revived in infinite transformations.

This vision was also shared by Giuseppe Abbati, who painted the *Interior of a Cloister* in Florence in 1861, when he was twenty-five. Less analytical than Borrani, Abbati was sensitive to the essence of form. By concentrating on those passages where the tension between light and shade was most acute, he sought images that contained within themselves the luminous power of nature. In his pictures, the things of the world seem to be arranged like presences on the stage of a sacred mystery, some emerging as epiphanies of light, others sinking into a shade that is nevertheless temporary, vibrating with a possible light, ready to shine again. Everything happens independently of human will and consciousness, which are transcended by light and shade: the little man has his back to the great blocks of marble, which the light brings to life but which he cannot see. The world is not just *res extensa*: the spirit of the world sings of the advent of the light, contemplating it with joy, in silence. There is more: while the man's awareness of the light is discontinuous, confined to moments of ecstatic openness, the things live on light, waiting for it in the dark, rejoicing in it in the sun. Contemplating them means, in the end, coming to resemble them, being like they are. This abandonment to the simple pleasure of existence is the condition for seeing the gods: a thought that, through Virgil and Horace, has nourished the Latin feeling for life right down to the present day.

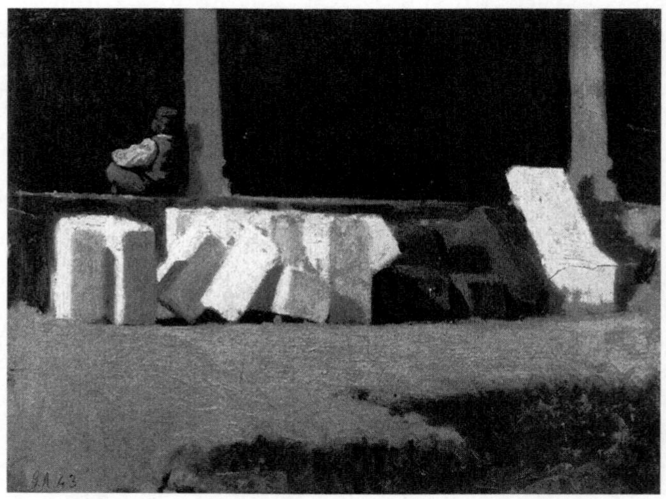

Giuseppe Abbati, Interior of a Cloister, 1861

The painting that was done in Tuscany in those years transformed the original neoplatonic vision of art at the same time as it evoked it, responding with the persuasive force of the images to the question that an expert on Plotinus, Pierre Hadot, still poses today: 'Cannot the ineffable, the mysterious, the transcendent, even the Absolute, also be discovered in the inexhaustible richness of the present moment and in the contemplation of the most concrete, banal, everyday, humble, immediate reality? And cannot the always-present Presence be sensed in it? "Exclude all things", said Plotinus. Instead, in sharp contradiction, should we not also say: "Admit all things"?' (Hadot 1999, p.114).

The images of those small pictures resolve this paradox through a twofold operation of taking in and taking away: the sensible is intensified at some points and dissolved at others, leading to the revelation, to the gaze that re-creates it, the artist's gaze and our own, of precisely that Presence which is immanent in it. Perhaps it can be said that in the form attained in this way being has become aware of itself and at the same time has revealed itself, or rather that the invisible has found the space and the light in which to make itself visible.

This process, and the image in which it culminates, is clearly recognizable in the work of Giovanni Fattori, who painted *On the Lookout* in 1872, at the age of forty-seven. Here, as in other pictures of his, we find not so much ecstatic wonder as a sense of suspended tension. The horses, like the oxen in other paintings, appear to be pent up with a vital energy that is betrayed in minimal movements, about to be set loose.

Giovanni Fattori, On the Lookout, 1972

And this extends to the men, to their faces, thrust slightly forward, to their gestures, barely hinted at, and above all to the intensity of their expressions, even though concealed in shadow. An almost frozen dance, which the oblique cut of the scene both contains and orients in predictable movements: in fact the orthogonal lines in the background provide a stability that the slanting lines at once reveal to be precarious.

Here the other Apollonian quality is added to the light that pervades and transfigures, a cosmic music to which everything seems to be silently attuned. The world is pervaded by a rhythm on which the animals are intent and to which they move, thereby weaving the immanent harmony and rendering it visible.

The cosmic music modulates the emotions that pass through the soul of the world and percolate into the human spirit: harmonizing with this music is all the more necessary for those artists who, like Fattori, give voice to the humble toil of life and the anguish of the world. In *Abandoned Soldiers,* painted in 1870, the bodies of two dead men are beginning to sink into the earth, which opens to receive them. The orthogonal lines that suspend the movement elsewhere have vanished; to the immobility of death responds an accord of oblique lines, which direct the observer's gaze downward: the horizon slopes downwards, the crowns of the pine and the more distant trees slope downwards, while the broad unsurfaced road seems to carry the bodies down with it, flowing like a river. Everything is viewed from below, in a foreshortening that is reminiscent of Mantegna's *Dead Christ*.

Giovanni Fattori, Abandoned Soldiers, 1870

The slightly rippling horizon is the silent protagonist of the picture. Everything is related to it, everything is directed towards it, even the grief, which is finally assuaged in it: the horizon, where sky and earth, death and life, personal sorrow and sorrow of the world permeate one another and coexist. This, simply this, is 'beauty', the harmony in which the otherwise discordant sounds of the world, of the soul, are attuned; and it is contemplating the world with a lover's heart, as Plotinus would have put it, that reveals the beauty to the senses and allows the imagination to conjure it up, to recollect it. The beauty that presents itself, and can present itself, only here and now: in this moment, on this earth, in this life.

Silvestro Lega was able to see it, in his *Mazzini on his Deathbed*, even at the moment when an individual life is drawing to its close. He painted this picture at a time of grief, in 1873, when he was forty-seven and had just lost both the woman he loved and his closest friends, Sernesi and Abbati.

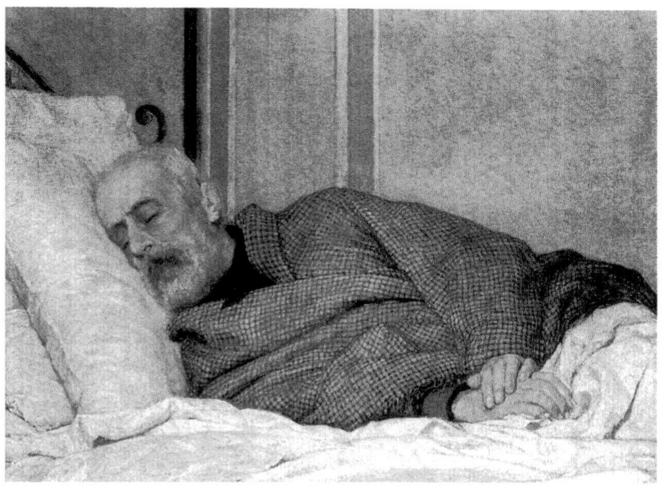

Silvestro Lega, Mazzini on his Deathbed, 1873

A few months earlier he had rushed to Pisa, to the bedside of the old champion of the republic whom he, like many other patriots, regarded not just as a political leader but also as a spiritual guide. Mazzini had taken refuge in Pisa to escape the hostility of the monarchic authorities, and was dying. Seated next to him and watching him, Lega may have eased his sorrow by drawing the beloved features. An artist who had always been so attentive to the grace of feminine gestures, to interiors and the quiet life of the home, he was now contemplating the naked simplicity of his master, lying on his deathbed.

He took the idea of the picture from those sketches, and painted it in sober colours, in small and soft touches that lend a subtle vibration to the brushwork. The light appears subdued, reflected from the cushions, from the sheet in which the old man is wrapped, and reverberating gently on the face. The body of the dying man is shown close-up, life-size; the wall behind him seems to support him and almost push him forwards; there is no perspective to place him at a distance, and so we too find ourselves at his bedside. He is lying on one side as if asleep, trusting in those who tend him, his hands at rest, inviting us to place our own on them with devotion.

We can discern in this image the harmony of a form achieved, the 'beautiful old man', the *kalogeros* of the ancients. In him the invisible has slowly come to the surface over the course of the years, finally reaching its full splendour—*splendor formae* was the medieval definition of beauty. The invisible has now become transparent and visible in a detail, in that unique form, in the mortal called Giuseppe Mazzini.

In the prologue to his memoirs, Jung wrote: 'In the end the only events in my life worth telling are those when the imperishable world irrupted into this transitory one' (Jung 1963, p.18). And in a later chapter: '... my works are a more or less successful endeavour to incorporate this incandescent matter into the contemporary picture of the world' (Jung 1963, p.225). When he wrote Freud's obituary in 1939, he made use of similar metaphors: '... he was a man possessed by a daemon—a man who had been vouchsafed an overwhelming revelation that took possession of his soul and never let him go' (Jung 1966,4, par. 71). And at the Eranos conference of the following year he had written: 'And because individuation is an heroic and often tragic task, the most difficult of all, it involves suffering, a *passion of the ego*. The ordinary, empirical man we once were is burdened with the fate of losing himself in a greater dimension and being robbed of his fancied freedom of will. He suffers, so to speak, from the violence done to him by the Self.' (Jung 1958,2, par. 233). There can be no better summary of a psychoanalytical theory that is an elaboration of an experience of the sublime. Expressions like 'irrupted', 'revelation', 'passion' and 'violence' suggest that at the root of this experience there is a split that isolates and confines the ego, separating it from a boundless world, from a surrounding mystery that is at once fearful and fascinating. It is precisely to this world that Friedrich's figures seem to turn, staring into the distance, immobile in the face of the void that gapes before them.

There is no void or unbridgeable distance, however, in the work of the Tuscan painters. In the 'land where lemons bloom', as Goethe called Italy (*Wilhelm Meister's Apprenticeship*, Book III, Chap. 1), the gods are not the disturbing 'Absolutely Other', but walk alongside human beings, even when they are not aware of it. They visit them freely, like Jupiter and Mercury visited Philemon and Baucis, and ask only to be received as guests. The house of analysis, in this land of images, is that of the aging couple, where men and gods meet and converse around a table, where the images that arrive are memory of the invisible, revelation of an eternal presence. There is no irruption of the 'numinous' to break down bastions, but a slow progress from the formless and inharmonious towards form, which grows more and more defined as the gaze becomes more attentive, the sensibility more refined, until the divine is unveiled: the gods are hidden, not separate, and reveal themselves to those who welcome them with *pietas*. 'All things are full of gods', it has been said, and beauty is the manifestation of this, every day and everywhere, even in a gesture, an image, a word; and yet evident only to those who are driven by the ardent energy of Amor, the immortal son of Venus. While her mortal son, we recall here in conclusion, was the *pius* Aeneas, mythical ancestor of Rome, who had Venus to guide him in the world and who was himself a bridge between past and future.

REFERENCES

Alberto Magno (1980). *De Natura Loci,* in Hossfeld, P. (Ed.), *Opera ominia,* 2 vols. Münster: Aschendorff.

Arcangeli, F. (1981). *Giorgio Morandi.* Turin: Einaudi.

Aristotle. *De Anima.* Ross, D. (Ed.). Oxford: Oxford University Press 1956 [reprinted 1991].

Baboni, A. and Cortenova, G. (Eds.) (1998). *Giovanni Fattori.* Milan: Electa.

Barasch, M. (2000). *Theories of Art, Volume 2. From Winckelmann to Baudelaire.* New York: Routledge.

Berger, J. (1996). *Splendori e miserie di Pablo Picasso.* Milan: Il Saggiatore.

Briganti, G. and Coen, E. (1984). *I paesaggi di Morandi.* Turin:Allemandi.

Carus, C.G. (1972). *Briefe über Landschaftsmalerei.* Heidelberg: L. Schneider.

Coomaraswamy, A.K. (1946). *Figures of Speech or Figures of Thought?* London: Luzrac & Co.

Corbin, H. (1969). *Alone with the Alone. Creative Imagination in the Sūfism of Ibn 'Arabī.* Princeton: Princeton University Press [Reprinted with a new preface by H. Bloom, Chichester: Princeton University Press, 1997].

Corbin, H. (1973). "Mysticism and Humour", Schroader, C.E. (Trans.), in *Spring* (1973), pp. 24–34.

Dante Alighieri (1995). *Convivio*. Vasoli, C. and De Robertis, D. (Eds.). *Opere Minori*, 2 vols. Milan-Naples: Riccardo Ricciardi.

Dini, F. (Ed.) (2002). *I Macchiaioli. Opere e protagonisti di una rivoluzione artistica* (1861–1869). Florence: Pagliai Polistampa.

Durbé, D. Ed. (1976). *I Macchiaioli.* Centro Di: Florence.

Eliade, M. (1989). *Shamanism.* London: Penguin Books.

Ellenberger, H.F. (1970). *The Discovery of the Unconscious.* New York: Basic Books.

Euripides. *Andromache,* in Kovacs, D. (Ed. & Trans.). *Euripides, Vol. II: Children of Heracles: Hippolytus, Andromache, Hecuba.* Cambridge, Mass. & London: Harvard University Press, 1996.

Freud, S. (1916a). "On transience". *On the History of the Psycho-Analytic Movement and Other Works.* S. E., *14*: 305–07. London: The Hogarth Press.

Freud, S. (1923b). *The Ego and the Id.* S. E. 19. London: The Hogarth Press.

Freud, S. (1933a). *New Introductory Lectures on Psycho-Analysis.* S. E., 22. London: The Hogarth Press.

Gaillard, C. (1998). *Le Musée Imaginaire d e Carl Gustav Jung.* Baume-les-Dames: Éditions Stock.

Goethe, J.W. (1976). *Faust.* Hamlin, C. (Ed.) & Arndt, W. (Trans.). New York & London: W.W. Norton & Company.

Goethe, J.W. (1970). *Italian Journey [1786–1788].* Auden, W.H. and Mayer, E. (Trans.). London: Penguin Books.

Goethe, J.W. (1989/1995). *Wilhelm Meister's Apprenticeship. Goethe The Collected Works,* Volume 9. Blackall, E.A. (Ed. and Trans.), in cooperation with V. Lange. Princeton: Princeton University Press.

Guntrip, H.J.S. (1968). *Schizoid Phrnomena, Object-Relations, and the Self.* London: Hogarth Press.

Hillman, J. (1971). "Psychology: monotheistic or polytheistic?" *Spring,* 193–208, 230–32.

Hillman, J. (1972). "Failure and analysis." *Journal of Analytical Psychology. 17*: 1–6 [reprinted in *Loose Ends,* pp. 98–104. Dallas, Texas: Spring Publications 1975].

Hillman, J. (1973). "Plotino, Ficino, and Vico as precursors of archetypal psychology". In *Loose Ends* (pp. 146–169). Dallas, Texas: Spring Publications 1975.

Hillman (1983). *Archetypal Psychology. A Brief Account.* Dallas: Spring Publications [reprinted Woodstock: Spring Publications, Inc., 1997].

Hillman, J. (1984). *The Thought of the Heart.* Eranos Lecture Series 2. Dallas: Spring Publications.

Hillman, J. (1993). "Alchemical blue and the unio mentalis." *Spring 54,* 132–48.

Hesiod. *Theogony,* in Wender, D. (Trans.), *Hesiod and Theognis*. London: Penguin Books 1973.

Hofstadter, A. (1971). *Martin Heidegger, Poetry, Language, Thought.* New York: Harper Colophon Books.

Hölderlin, F. (1966). *Poems and Fragments.* Hamburger, M. (Trans.). London: Routledge & Kegan Paul Ltd. [Fourth Edition London: Anvil Press Poetry Ltd 2004].

Homer. *The Iliad*. Rieu, E.V. (Trans.). Harmondsworth: Penguin Books 1950.

Homer *The Odyssey.* Cook, A. (Ed. & Trans.). New York & London: Norton & Company.

Homeric Hymns (1970). *The Homeric Hymns.* Boer, C. (Trans.). Dallas: Spring Publications, 6th Printing 1993.

Hadot, P. (1988), "La figura di Socrate". In *Esercizi spirituali e filosofia antica.* Turin: Einaudi.

Hadot, P. (1999). *Platino o la semplicità dello sguardo*. Turin: Einaudi.

Jonas, H. (1987). "The concept of God after Auschwitz". In *Mortality and Morality: Search for the Good after Auschwitz* Vogel, L. (Ed.). Chicago: Northwestern University Press, 1996.

Jung, C.G. ([1916]/1957). "The transcendent function". *The Structure and Dynamics of the Psyche.* C.E., *8*: 67–91. London: Routledge & Kegan Paul.

Jung, C.G. (1916b). *Psychology of the Unconscious. A Study on the Transformation and Symbolisms of the Libido. A Contribution to the History of the Evolution of Thought*. London: Kegan Paul, Trench, Trubner [Reprinted London: Routledge 1991].

Jung, C.G. (1921)/1971). *Psychological Types*. C.W., 6. London: Routledge & Kegan Paul.

Jung, C.G. (1925a) *VII Sermones ad Mortuos. The Seven Sermons to the Dead Written by Basilides in Alexandria, the City Where the East Toucheth the West.* Edinburgh: Neill.

Jung, C.W. (1931a, 3). "On the relation of analytical psychology to poetry". *The Spirit in Man, Art, and Literature.* C.W., *15*: 65–83. London: Routledge & Kegan Paul.

Jung, C.G. (1933a, 9). "Basic postulates of analytical psychology". *The Structure and Dynamics of the Psyche.* C.W., *8*: 338–57. London: Routledge & Kegan Paul.

Jung, C.G. (1939b). "The dreamlike world of India". *Civilization in Transition*. C.W., *10*: 515–24. London: Routledge & Kegan Paul.

Jung, C. G. (1946c). "The psychology of the transference". *The Practice of Psychotherapy. Essays on the Psychology of the Transference and Other Subjects*. C.W., *16*: 163–321. London: Routledge & Kegan Paul.

Jung, C.G. (1948a, 2). "The phenomenology of the spirit in fairytales." *The Archetypes of the Collective Unconscious*. C.W., *9,1*: 384–455. London: Routledge & Kegan Paul.

Jung, C.G. (1948a, 4). "A psychological approach to the dogma of the Trinity". *Psychology and Religion: West and East*. C.W., *11*: 107–200. London: Routledge & Kegan Paul.

Jung, C.G. (1953). *Psychology and Alchemy*. London: Routledge & Kegan Paul.

Jung, C.G. (1954). "Analytical psychology and education". *The Development of Personality*. C.W., *17*: 63–132. London: Routledge & Kegan Paul.

Jung, C.G. (1954b, 2). "On the nature of the psyche". *The Structure and Dynamics of the Psyche* C.W., *8*: pp. 159–234. London: Routledge & Kegan Paul.

Jung, C.G. (1955b). "Transformation symbolism in the Mass". *Psychology and Religion: West and East*. C.W., *11*: 201–96. London: Routledge & Kegan Paul.

Jung, C.G. (1956). *Symbols of Transformation. An Analysis of the Prelude to a Case of Schizophrenia*. C.W., 5. London: Routledge & Kegan Paul.

Jung, C.G. (1958, 2). "A psychological approach to the dogma of the Trinity." *Psychology and Religion: West and East*. C.W., *11*: 107–200. London: Routledge & Kegan Paul.

Jung, C.G. (1959). *Aion: Researches into the Phenomenology of the Self*. C.W., 9, ii. London: Routledge & Kegan Paul.

Jung, C.G. (1963). *Memories, Dreams, Reflections*. London: Collins and Routledge & Kegan Paul. [Reprinted London: Fontana Paperbacks, 1983.]

Jung, C.G. (1963). *Mysterium Coniunctionis. An Inquiry into the Separation and Synthesis of Psychic Opposites in Alchemy*. C.W., 14. London: Routledge & Kegan Paul.

Jung, G.C. (1966, 4). "In Memory of Sigmund Freud." *The Spirit in Man, Art, and Literature*. C.W., *15*: 60–73. London: Routledge & Kegan Paul.

Jung, C.G. (1966, 6). "On the relation of analytical psychology to poetry." *The Spirit in Man, Art, and Literature*. C.W., *15*: 65–83. London: Routledge & Kegan Paul.

Jung, C.G. (1966, 7). "Psychology and literature." *The Spirit in Man, Art, and Literature.* C.W., *15*: 84–105. London: Routledge & Kegan Paul.

Jung, C.G. (1967). *Alchemical Studies.* C.W., 13. London: Routledge & Kegan Paul.

Jung, C.G. (1976a). *Letters. Volume 2:* 1951–1961. Gerhard Adler, A. and Jaffé, A. (Eds.). London: Routledge & Kegan Paul.

Kierkegaard, S. (1972). "Briciole di filosofia." *Opere.* Fabro, D. (Ed.), Florence: Sansoni.

Koerner, J.L. (1990). *Caspar David Friedrich and the Subject of Landscape.* New Haven and London: Yale University Press.

Levi D'Ancona, M. (1983). *Botticelli's Primavera: A Botanical interpretation including Astrology, Alchemy and the Medici.* Florence: Olschki.

Levi, P. (1992). *Zoran Music. Dialogo con l'autoritratto.* Milan: Electa.

Magnani, L. (1982). *Il mio Morandi.* Turin: Einaudi.

Matteucci, G., Monti, R., Sisi, C. and Steingräber, E., (Eds.) (1991). *Gli anni di Piagentina. Natura e forma nell'arte dei Macchiaioli.* Florence: Artificio.

Mazzocca, F. and Sisi, C. (2003). *I Macchiaioli prima dell'impressionismo.* Venice: Marsilio.

Zoran Music. Milan: Electa, 1992.

Zoran Music. Paris: Réunion des Musées Nationaux, 1995.

Peppiatt, M. (2000a). *Zoran Music.* Norwich: Sainsbury Centre for Visual Arts.

Peppiatt, M. (2000b). *Zoran Music: Entretiens 1988–1998.* Paris: L'échoppe.

Pessoa, F. (1984). *Una sola moltitudine.* Milan: Adelphi.

Pessoa, F. (1998). *Fernando Pessoa & Co.: Selected Poems,* Zenith, R. (Ed. and Trans.) New York: Grove Press.

Pessoa, F. (2005). *Le poesie di Ricardo Reis,* Florence: Passigli.

Panofsky, E. (1962). *Studies in Iconology. Humanistic Themes in the Art of the Renaissance.* London: Benjamin Nelson [Republished New York, Hagerstown, San Francisco, London: Icon Editions, 1972].

Orifici (1968). *Frammenti.* Turin: Boringhieri.

Pico della Mirandola (1994). *Commento sopra una canzona d'amore.* De Angelis, P. (Ed.). Palermo: Novecento.

Plato. *Alcibiades.* Denver, N. (Ed.) Cambridge: Trinity College, 2001.

Plato. *Cratylus.* In: Hamilton, E. & Cairns, H. (Eds.) (1961). *The Collected Dialogues of Plato.* Princeton: Princeton University Press.

Plato. *Laws.* In: Hamilton, E. & Cairns, H. (Eds.) (1961). *The Collected Dialogues of Plato.* Princeton: Princeton University Press.

Plato. *Phaedrus*. In: Hamilton, E. & Cairns, H. (Eds.) (1961). *The Collected Dialogues of Plato*. Princeton: Princeton University Press.

Plato. *Symposium*. In: Hamilton, E. & Cairns, H. (Eds.) (1961). *The Collected Dialogues of Plato*. Princeton: Princeton University Press.

Plato. *Timaeus*. In: Hamilton, E. & Cairns, H. (Eds.) (1961). *The Collected Dialogues of Plato*. Princeton: Princeton University Press.

Plotinus. *Enneads*. Armstrong, A.H. (Trans.), Vols. I–VII. Cambridge, Mass. & London: Harvard University Press, 1966–1988.

Santini, P.C. (1984). "Boschi come paesaggi dell'anima". In *Nei boschi e altri dipinti*. Prato: Galleria Metastasio.

Santini, P.C. (1984). "L'opera di Carlo Mattioli". In *Carlo Mattioli. Opere 1944–1984*. Milan: Olivetti.

Sala, C. (1994). *Caspar David Friedrich and Romantic Painting*. Paris: Éditions Pierre Terrail.

Semerano, G. (2004). *L'infinito: un equivoco millenario*. Milan: Bruni Mondadori.

Stein, I. (1917). *Zum Problem der Einfühlung*. Halle: Buchdrucheri des Waisenhauses. [*On the Problem of Empathy*. Stein, W. (Trans.). Collected Works of Edith Stein 3 (1989). Washington, D.C.: Institute of Carmelite Studies].

St. Thomas Aquinas (1948). *Summa Theologica*. New York: Benziger Bros.

Suhrawardî, S.Y. (1976). *L'archange empourpré*. Corbin, H. (Trans.). Paris: Fayard.

Terrasse, A. (1984). "Les notes de Bonnard". In *Bonnard*. Centre Georges Pompidou, Paris.

Vaughan, W. (1980/1994). *German Romantic Painting* (2nd Edition). London and New Haven: Yale.

Weisel, E. (1981). *Night*. London: Penguin 1981.

Wind, E. (1967). *Pagan Mysteries in the Renaissance*. Harmondsworth: Peregrine Books.

Wolf, N. (2003). *Caspar David Friedrich*. London: Taschen.

INDEX